STEPHEN WILLATS

STEPHEN WILLATS

Between Buildings and People

A.D. ACADEMY EDITIONS

First published in Great Britain in 1996 by
ACADEMY EDITIONS
an imprint of

ACADEMY GROUP LTD
42 Leinster Gardens, London W2 3AN
Member of the VCH Publishing Group

ISBN: 1 85490 436 1

Distributed to the trade in the United States of America by
NATIONAL BOOK NETWORK, INC
4720 Boston Way, Lanham, Maryland 20706

Printed and bound in Singapore

CONTENTS

Introduction   6

The Emergence of a New Reality   22

An Island Within an Island   32

Pat Purdy and the Glue-Sniffers' Camp   58

Taboo Housing Estate   66

What Is He Trying To Get At? Where Does He Want To Go?   72

Difficult Boy in a Concrete Block   80

Sitting Between Two Desks   86

Inside The Space We Have Been Given   94

Sorting Out Other People's Lives   100

Brentford Towers   108

From a Walk to the Supermarket   124

Signs and Messages from Corporate America   130

Personal Islands   136

Bibliography   144

Introduction

The idea of a structure being composed of structural series of elements which determine the overall shape and function also creating an internal environment, is the construction in all natural phenomena, an ideal example being the cell. In the cell one has a number of elements which are working towards a function and the whole. Similarly, the architectural designer has a set of elements which limit the design possibility. He uses a set of elements; the room, corridor, hall, etc. each element having a function and also limiting the visual structure of the whole. The architectural designer's vision is conceived within the limitation of the materials and the structural elements. (1961)

Every second of every day that I perceive the urban landscape I am bombarded with messages from the outface of the society from which it originated. My simple progress down any street is an encounter with a complex mosaic of signs, all of which exert some form of influence on my actions, and my cognition of events.

This multi-channel bombardment comes at me from all angles and frequencies, and would surely be an overwhelmingly random event if I were not able to filter out what I want to accept. This selective attention effectively positions those signs into a competitive juxtaposition with my priorities, with my actual movement generating a state of flux in what is being actively cognised at any particular moment. There is a shifting hierarchy of what focuses my attention, and what will be extracted by me from a background of signs that all denote in some way the past, present and future. Thus some signs are the residue of past behaviour and inform me of what might have been, others direct and condition my current acts, and still others give me a sense of what might or could happen, providing a psychological framework for approaching the future.

Right at the outset of my involvement with the structural form of modern building in the early 1960s, I realised their relationship with social ideology (*above*). For the form of our physical environment is part of the background mosaic of signs encountered in our daily lives. The building and architecture of any street is also an expression of the ideology driving society. In their physical form and fabric, buildings contain both the idealisations and pragmatics of how society sees itself, as well as the consciousness that exists between people themselves and the conventions that govern the way those exchanges happen. It is against the architectural backdrop of other people's plans that I continue my daily life, and the more all-embracing and formally constructed this is, the greater the intended influence on my attitudes, beliefs and behaviour.

Even the material fabric of the building that contains my behaviour exerts an influence over me. The walls of the room I sit in contain a very different message if they are made of wood as opposed to concrete. But the message of buildings is inescapably institutional, and as such, reflects the determinism inherent in the role of the institution in providing order and certainty.

The provision of certainty is an important parameter to the creation of culture, and we look to the institutional agencies of culture to provide us with models of what will be probable – amongst the possible – in the entropic chaos inherent in daily life. Buildings give us all certainty.

I was drawn to Modernist buildings in the early 1960s for they were huge, monumental structures that dwarfed most of the preceding architecture. At that time they indicated an optimistic view of a mutual liberal society freed from the constraining taboos of the 1950s.

These buildings in particular are overtly conceived cultural icons, developed as expressions which demonstrate an idealised order; the physicality of the building's form reflects society's outlook towards the norms and conventions of interpersonal behaviour. But at the same time there is an unyielding determinism inherent in what building has come to represent, which requires me to adapt my behaviour in relation to what has been planned, and to accommodate what I encounter within my own psychological realm. Integral to the cultural fabric of signs are the personal displays we all make as an outface of our own self-organisation and drive for identity, which leads us into making a contextual layering of our creative potential on to the fabric of the building. So while the message stemming from the fabric of the building plan is essentially reductive and object-based, in contrast, the language of its actual occupation by people is rich and complex.

A building is an outface of the institutional fabric of society, but within, it is also an expression of the self-organisation in people's lives. It is this dynamic which has formed a central part of my strategy of locating my art practice in territories that are meaningful and accessible to the audience of my works. This idea has been taken forward to a point where I consider that the audience of the work of art is as important as the artist, and that the active involvement of people in the origination of art work is an essential part of the process of generating interventions in the social process of culture. This notion of intervention is important to the artist breaking through existing norms and conventions to establish new perceptions of what culture might be, to give cultural heuristics for the future.

Consequently, my engagement with buildings in the general strategy of my work has

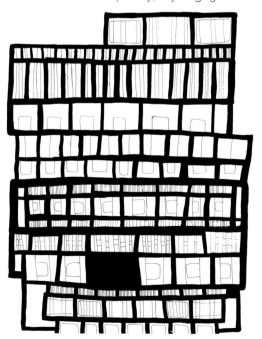

been tactical, and as a result I have identified some buildings rather than others as clearly demonstrating this polemic – these are the ones I have been drawn towards. This has certainly been the case with those 'Modernist' building programmes for residential accommodation and offices (*left*) that took place from the end of the 1960s to the middle of the 1970s. This large-scale construction resulted in buildings that were stereotypes of what Modernism could mean. They were not the original conception, validated by architectural practices as masterpieces of design, but were more an emulation. Even while they were being constructed en masse I considered that the context of these Modernist

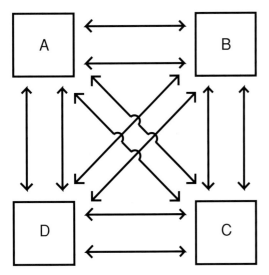

buildings provided me with a language and an associated world of meaning that would be available to an audience, for even if they had never lived in such a building themselves, all would be aware of their ramifications in contemporary life. This made me hunt for those buildings I thought might form a context for a possible work, which could act as a catalyst for externalising the basic concept of self-organisation in my practice.

As an abstraction, self-organisation is the notion of a system (*left*) determining its own parts and how each part behaves in relation to the other. As an actuality affecting the way we live, it is expressed in the basic drive to create one's own order, both psychologically and interpersonally, and to project it on to what is there, leading to an inherent relativity in perception. Such a drive to express the existence of the self is in implicit opposition to the universal determinism inherent in the reductions made by institutional society. It therefore exists as a counter-consciousness often in a marginal or coexisting relationship with those dominant norms.

A considerable part of the rationale behind my practice has been to consider how the artwork might intervene in the fabric of culture. Consequently, I do not see any reason why a work of art has to be held – as it has come to be held – within the institutional domain of art galleries and museums. This belief is consistent with the manifestation of self-organisation, for I consider that the institutional domain of art has become separated from the general flux and priorities of people's daily lives. Now exclusive and authoritative, it relies on the audience being already versed in its internal languages and academic pursuits. I saw that a much more meaningful communication could take place if works were developed within the existing structure of people's lives. Thus the reality of the audience was immediately emphasised, and the concept forwarded in the work contextualised into their existing frame of reference and social behaviours.

In order for this externalisation of the work into society to take place, I have evolved a model of practice based on experience that effectively encompasses the very different environmental and social conditions that exist outside the art museum. While from the late 1950s I had speculated on various ways of approaching the museum as an interactive space, and had made participatory wall constructions and clothing works, it all led to a point where the confines of the museum were becoming claustrophobic, stifling the spirit of availability and externalisation towards a more available, open kind of art practice. In 1965 I initiated my first experimental work, assisted by a group of students from Ipswich Art School on a housing estate for London 'overspill' located on the outskirts of Ipswich. From the outset it became obvious that a model of practice would be required that would bind it to the context in which the artwork was to be presented, and which could embody the priorities, languages and behaviours of the audience. The existing language of the audience became a paramount issue in this new relationship. By using it as the language of the work, I thought a more immediate, less inhibited engagement would be possible with people that did not normally spend time attending to contemporary art.

During the latter part of the 1960s I further developed my thinking into a methodology that resulted in such conceptual works as *Man From The Twenty-First Century*[1] and *The Social Resource Project For Tennis Clubs*,[2] (*below*) and this formulation was behind the framework of procedures devised for *West London Social Resource Project* (1972-73). It was principally this work which led to my engagement with people and the buildings they inhabit, thus exploring a relationship between the social reality they construct and the physical environment.

In its conception, *West London Social Resource Project* was seen as an expression of self-organisation, and in an abstract form was a dynamic model comprising a sequence of events in time. These events would be manifest within the daily lives of people – the audience – though here they were to be seen more fully as participants. By making this move beyond the institutional boundaries of art, much of what has been taken for granted has to be rethought, and the composition of the audience becomes a very basic concern, especially if relevant decisions about context and language are to be pursued.

Thus in my planning of the work, four social groupings were specified as typically representative of English contemporary society at that time. These were located in small neighbourhoods in Harrow, West Ealing, Greenford and Osterley. As they were economically, socially and physically separated from each other, one aim of the work was to create an engagement between them. I started a search for the four groupings, travelling around West London (chosen because of its accessibility to where I lived) looking for distinct, but still typical social groupings, in contexts which, although contained, would also be physically accessible for each group.

In looking for these particular contexts, various practical aspects became deciding criteria. For example, the areas had to be small enough to be handled by an administrative team of four voluntary project operators, and their size would enable a significant presence to be made by the work. Consequently, we identified neighbourhoods that were architecturally defined, bound by environmental features, such as a road, canal or park, and comprising a few interconnected streets with local resources, such as shops and libraries.

I then went about building up a contextual framework of photographed images taken from each area, for example items taken from the garden, fronts of houses and street signs. I placed a special emphasis on objects that represented a counter-consciousness of self-organisation hidden amongst the fabric of deterministic signs. These sets of objects and signs were then embodied in two small books that became the active agency in the structure of the work. It was essentially in two parts, using the books to present residents with a sequence of questions about the

SOCIAL RESOURCE PROJECT FOR TENNIS CLUBS, TENNIS SUPER GIRL POSTER NO 9

SOCIAL RESOURCE PROJECT FOR TENNIS CLUBS, TENNIS SUPER GIRL POSTER NO 5

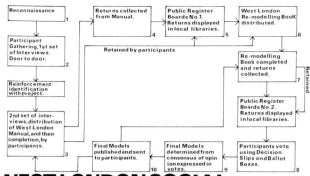

WEST LONDON SOCIAL RESOURCE PROJECT

Flow diagram:

1. Reconnaissance
2. Participant Gathering, 1st set of Interviews. Door to door.
   - Reinforcement identification with project.
3. 2nd set of interviews, distribution of West London Manual, and their completion, by participants.
4. Returns collected from Manual.
5. Public Register Boards No.1. Returns displayed in local libraries.
6. West London Re-modelling Book distributed.
7. Re-modelling Book completed and returns collected.
8. Public Register Boards No.2. Returns displayed in local libraries.
   - Participants vote using Decision Slips and Ballot Boxes.
9. Final Models determined from consensus of opinion expressed in votes.
10. Final Models published and sent to participants.

Retained by participants — Retained

WEST LONDON SOCIAL RESOURCE PROJECT

The West London Social Resource Project attempts to determine what social/physical environment you and the community in the area you live in see as serving your actual needs.

Initially it asks you to examine your existing environment in order to ascertain what perceptions, attitudes, behaviours exist, and at what level does it relate to your needs. The project also shows you how other people in three different areas in West London feel about their environment, and their proposals for one built around what they consider their needs to be.

Thus it helps you obtain insight, understanding in to the environment you live in, showing how you relate to it, and how it relates to others.

WEST LONDON WASTE LANDS

AREA ONE

WEST LONDON SOCIAL RESOURCE PROJECT

The West London Social Resource Project attempts to determine what social/physical environment you and the community in the area you live in see as serving your actual needs.

Initially it asks you to examine your existing environment in order to ascertain what perceptions, attitudes, behaviours exist, and at what level does it relate to your needs. The project also shows you how other people in three different areas in West London feel about their environment, and their proposals for one built around what they consider their needs to be.

Thus it helps you obtain insight, understanding in to the environment you live in, showing how you relate to it, and how it relates to others.

WEST LONDON WASTE LANDS

AREA TWO

WEST LONDON SOCIAL RESOURCE PROJECT

The West London Social Resource Project attempts to determine what social/physical environment you and the community in the area you live in see as serving your actual needs.

Initially it asks you to examine your existing environment in order to ascertain what perceptions, attitudes, behaviours exist, and at what level does it relate to your needs. The project also shows you how other people in three different areas in West London feel about their environment, and their proposals for one built around what they consider their needs to be.

Thus it helps you obtain insight, understanding of your environment, showing how you relate to it, and how it relates to others.

WEST LONDON WASTE LANDS

AREA THREE

WEST LONDON SOCIAL RESOURCE PROJECT

The West London Social Resource Project attempts to determine what social/physical environment you and the community in the area you live in see as serving your actual needs.

Initially it asks you to examine your existing environment in order to ascertain what perceptions, attitudes, behaviours exist, and at what level does it relate to your needs. The project also shows you how other people in three different areas in West London feel about their environment, and their proposals for one built around what they consider their needs to be.

Thus it helps you obtain insight, understanding of your environment, showing how you relate to it, and how it relates to others.

WEST LONDON WASTE LANDS

AREA FOUR

WEST LONDON SOCIAL RESOURCE PROJECT. (PUBLIC REGISTER BOARD NO.1)

fabric of their neighbourhood. The first book, *The West London Manual*, centred on presenting 'descriptive questions' on how people saw the things I had photographed in each area. The second, *The West London Remodelling Book*, posed 'prescriptive questions' on how people might want to change their environment. While the questions related to contextual sets of images built up from each neighbourhood in a way which was already meaningful, responses could be made in an open frame, so that any response was a complete interpretative expression by each individual participant. Purposefully, there was no evaluative criteria made in the structure of the work; each response was as valid as another, it being left to residents to make their own evaluations and connections.

This open manifestation was achieved by displaying the responses from all four neighbourhoods on public register boards located in branch libraries, one in each area. This meant that everyone could compare the responses from their own neighbourhood with those of the others. I have made a more complete analysis of this project (*left*) elsewhere,[3] but one of the reasons for its significant impact on people's lives in the four neighbourhoods was undoubtedly due to the manner in which the work was contextualised into the social and physical fabric of those environments.

Questions that elicited much response centred on the representation and placement of personal objects in a participant's living room, and the immediate exterior of their house; the facade and front garden. When constructing these particular questions, I associated them with images of objects and signs that were a 'restricted code'[4]. This meant that they were derived from their connection with a specific event, routine or place, which would bring about an immediate recognition. Because of this dependence between the restricted code and prior experience, a vastly reduced set of signs can refer to a wide, complex realm of behaviour. By using images I knew already had a special meaning to local residents as a restricted code, I could unlock complex cognitive realms that would normally be excluded by inhibitions from expression and speculation.

The preparation of the *Manual* and the *Remodelling Book*, and the administration of people's responses to the questions contained therein, brought me to the realisation that there are objects which people position in their living environments as expressions of themselves, and there are also objects which represent society's institutional determinism in that space. Both are categories of expression and although possibly widely different, can live in a tolerated coexistence. The possession and display of objects vests the space and the occupant with 'something' of the ideology behind those objects. In one sense they can be selected to reinforce the existing outlook of the occupant, giving a cultural ambience from the past, as well as the contemporary present and the future. In another very important sense, individual collections of objects can create for the possessor a new feeling of self that did not exist previously. This is especially true of objects reflecting some idea of the future, as expressed in the stylistic innovations of domestic household objects, such as clocks and radios, as well as in the new fabrics and textile designs. Of course, there are also objects with which the possessor externalises a cultural message about themselves into the public domain, such as clothing, a car, the front gate or front door. But it is with the domestic interior space that objects have an extra specific significance in the psychological realm of the possessor, for within they can present a world of certainty away from the entropic forces outside. Here again it is the polemical discrepancy that becomes important in the rationale of my engagement with buildings, that there is a conflict between the message radiated by the external physicality of the building, and people's daily lives inside.

Later in the 1970s I began another search for a symbol of modern contemporary building to embody in my work, that would be clearly polemical to an audience, contain the idea of people's self-organisation and be a development from the suburban housing complexes I had embodied in *West London Social Resource Project*. I undertook new reconnaissance trips around the outer fringes of West London, looking for the context that would extend the methodologies established in earlier works to involve more of the physicality of the context in the work's structure. During these trips, of which I made many, I had noticed residential tower blocks dotted around the landscape. There appeared to be no apparent reason for them that I could immediately see, other than as symbols of the future, as there seemed to be plenty of land available for quite different forms of building. At the same time I was struck by the feeling that, if symbolism became actuality, this was the building that typified the world within which most people were destined to live. It was therefore a very relevant place for a work of art to be situated that created a positive critique of that future. The tower blocks I looked at during my reconnaissance were usually surrounded by typical low-rise, often terraced, post-war council housing. In 1975 I became more specific and started the search for a recently-completed housing complex, large enough to form a consistent entity in itself, like a contained island that appeared visually separated from the surrounding environment.

After some weeks of looking at tower blocks throughout West London, it was a friend who had a mother living in a tower block in Hayes named Skeffington Court that directed my attention to the particular complex of Modernist buildings at Silverdale Road. I immediately responded to the prospect of working on this estate, with its mixture of low-rise slab blocks, and the centrally positioned tower of Skeffington Court, that emerges out of the raised walkways like a Neolithic monument. The whole interconnected complex structure of buildings and platforms is made from red brick and grey concrete. My experience of working there was the next major step in shaping my subsequent approach to working between buildings and people.

When in late 1976 I started seriously exploring the estate, tower blocks had not become heavily stigmatised in the minds of residents, who were generally glad to have been given a new flat, and were in an optimistic frame of mind about their future lives at Skeffington Court. However, I did record some doubts, even then, about what the physical structure of the building was going to mean for their everyday routines, such as shopping, fixing the car and recreation.

Having decided on this estate, I developed a model of the work's structure in time that was specifically focused on the layout of Skeffington Court, so the building itself became an integral part of the work. My intention was to externalise the relationship between the

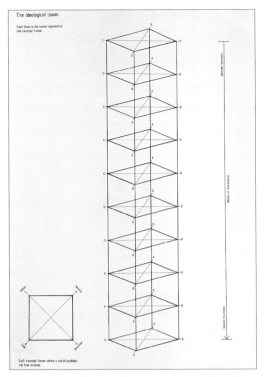

The ideological tower.

Each floor in the tower represents one concept frame.

Each concept frame views a social problem via four axioms.

building and people's lives, both descriptively (how things were), and prescriptively (how things should be), and in the process make a public statement of the counter-consciousness inherent inside this institutional symbol of determinism.

Vertical Living[5] formed a conceptual tower (*left*) inside Skeffington Court, which people constructed by their participation, loading it with contextual references pertinent to their daily lives. It consisted of a sequence of events facilitated by participation, thus causing the structure of the work to climb up inside the tower, floor by floor, from the bottom upwards. I wanted to make a strong link between the language of the work and its audience – the people who lived on the estate and immediately around, in order to facilitate access from their world, and to stimulate their involvement.

This led to my practice of inviting a small symbolic group, representative of the potential audience, to participate with me in the development of a work. The group would specifically define areas of meaning for me that it might centre upon, giving the work its references and language. With *Vertical Living*, my initial approach towards forming this symbolic group was to contact the caretaker at Skeffington Court who had his small office at the very bottom of the block, and my friend's mother who lived at the top. I discussed with them both the idea of the work and what I thought it might involve in an open way. I then asked them to think of people who might be interested in taking part, and subsequently to introduce them to me.

As I went on to meet more and more residents, I found they responded well to me and to the idea of *Vertical Living* – they were very willing to perceive it as a work of art. This didn't surprise me, for – as I had previously encountered – this was largely because here was something positive, that directly centred on what was already personally very meaningful. Also as one of the participants in *West London Social Resource Project* had commented, it was seen as putting something into the community, and not as taking anything away. In this respect the main question concerning the status as art of this and similar works of mine came from the art world, which though physically remote from the works, nevertheless felt threatened by their ramifications – the removal of the object, loss of status and the idea of a special territory for art. As a result it sought to marginalise their relevance by creating doubt as to what they might constitute as artwork.

My initial discussion with the caretaker quickly led to introductions to other residents of the tower, one person leading on to another, and while this took place over several weeks, I also stood at the entrance of the building, talking to people coming in and out about what I proposed. What I wanted to represent in the symbolic group were the various expectations

13

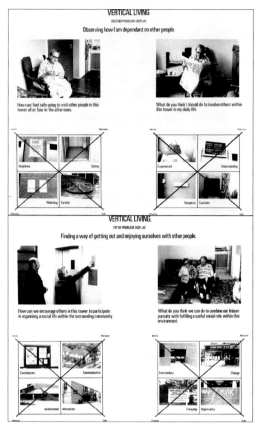

VERTICAL LIVING

SECOND PROBLEM DISPLAY.

Observing how I am dependant on other people.

How can I feel safe going to visit other people in this tower after four in the afternoon.

What do you think I should do to involve others within this tower in my daily life.

Neighbour / Safety

Experienced / Understanding

Watching / Careful

Receptive / Curiosity

VERTICAL LIVING.

FIFTH PROBLEM DISPLAY.

Finding a way of getting out and enjoying ourselves with other people.

How can we encourage others in this tower to participate in organising a social life within the surrounding community.

What do you think we can do to combine our leisure pursuits with fulfilling a useful social role within this environment.

Contributors / Communication

Intermediary / Change

Involvement / Interaction

Campaign / Opportunity

of residents, such as young newlyweds, single elderly pensioners and middle-aged working couples. As there was a council policy of no children in this block, family perceptions were already excluded. My approach was to discuss the idea of the work individually with residents, and then if they wanted to get involved, I would arrange a time with them to come back and formally start working together. I also asked each participant to introduce me to another resident they thought might be interested, and to come with me and explain to them what they had already been involved in creating.

This element of recognition of someone already familiar and from the same context was an invaluable factor in removing people's inhibitions and helping them make up their mind to participate. It also meant that the formation of the symbolic group was decided by the audience itself: I would accept whoever wanted to be a part of the group as long as they did not duplicate someone else already participating. A mutualistic relationship was immediately established that was further elaborated upon when I started working with people in the environment of their own flats.

My plan was for the conceptual tower to be formed from a sequence of display boards (*above*), consisting of photographs and texts defining a specific problem area, previously identified by an individual participant as reflecting their views about aspects of life in the tower. With each person I started from the situation of the living room, asking them to direct my camera to objects that they thought were significant to their life. I then made a tape-recorded discussion with them about their life in general terms, later transcribed into a text. After two weeks I returned, having looked at the transcript to ask the participant more specific questions around problem areas they might have identified. This might be the effect of the tower on working routines, weekend leisure pursuits, shopping, contact with friends, and so on. I then asked participants to identify objects within the flat environment, and signs in the environment immediately around the tower that they felt expressed something special about the problem area, and then asked them to direct my camera and frame an image of the subject they had found.

This process of developing contextual references was highly social, interactive and complex, taking about three months and many repeated visits to lead up to a point where the composition of the display boards could be fixed. It was the complicated social nature of an evolving relationship that propelled the work forward, with participants feeling more free to originate fresh insights, or at least ones they had not felt able to express before I met them. What became clear in this was the importance of the inside-outside relationship with the building; that the outside world had psychologically, as well as actually, formed an extension of the building that could be seen to be apparent and logical. Where this broke down, when it didn't make sense, an area of potential crisis was already becoming apparent to these new inhabitants, which undermined their optimism about their surroundings. The internal vertically segmented structure of the tower itself was under question, and its role in inhibiting relationships, internalising people within its fabric and distancing them from outside reality, was also beginning to be observed as a phenomenon by some of the residents as I made my documentation.

Even at this preparatory stage, what also began to emerge was an externalisation of what was normally hidden and implicit into a semi-formal structure: from the psychological realm of people who found themselves in a random juxtaposition to others in the same block. Residents had found themselves allocated to the tower block from a wide area around London for a variety of reasons, which meant that many were quite displaced and had to spend time attempting to orientate themselves within these new and unfamiliar surroundings. What I noticed, as with *West London Social Resource Project*, was that the objects people transported into the flat environment transformed the psychological realm of that space for the resident, and that this process of transformation was an act of creative self-organisation.

At the same time, the transported objects affected this anonymous and rigid space in a number of ways: they brought implicit references as to the origin of the resident into the space; they enlarged the psychological domain of the space to include aspects of the external world and gave that space an individual identity that was an extension of the resident's feelings about themselves. They also provided a capsule-like background reinforcement from the insecurity of the chaos outside and gave the resident an ideological frame of reference, an ambient climate of thinking about how they wanted to approach the future. As this was a very modern building, I was interested to see that younger residents developed their space with objects that had a unity with the architecture, while older residents' objects were in a more complex, and often conflicting relationship.

Having made the documentations, I then worked with the symbolic group to form the display boards, leaving the choice of visual and text references surrounding a problem area to be selected by the group, so that the work would essentially exhibit the feelings and perceptions of the audience. Each board presented a problem situation in the form of a question directed at the viewer of the board, which centred on a particular way of approaching the problem. Participants then developed conceptual solutions or responses to these questions within an open-frame format response sheet, one for each board. The completed sheets were collected and exhibited on a public register board situated directly opposite them on the landings of Skeffington Court. The display and register boards were freestanding, and of a size in proportion to the landing space outside the lifts, so as not to get in the way. They were also made in a manner that residents felt they could easily accomplish themselves; they were not too professionally polished or expensive looking.

Another very important factor in the acceptance of the display boards was for residents to feel that if they didn't like them they could easily remove them.

The impact of *Vertical Living* on life in the tower and the surrounding estate was profound – it completely opened up relationships between residents. People travelled from floor to floor to engage with the work, and in the process recognised people represented in the displays, bumped into neighbours and people who, perhaps, they just saw at a distance normally, creating a general discussion about what the work meant to them. Residents also met and welcomed people from outside the neighbourhood who came to view it, including artists, art critics, architects, social and community workers and participants from my other projects.

The impact and effect on relations within the tower was to override the isolating vertical structure and a feeling of community began to be created. Three weeks after the start of the installation, a meeting was called by residents and held in the foyer to discuss *Vertical Living* and people's impressions of being involved, an unimaginable event at the start of the work. The whole tower attended, and someone decided that they should walk through each others' flats to see what everyone had done in their own space. After the project had finished, some residents also decided to make their own display boards about issues of life within the tower, and for quite a few months they were to be found at the entrance of the building with images and texts made by themselves.

Another contributing factor to the work's continuing effect was that it was conceived as a total entity in time. There was a perceived beginning to the relationship of the work to the tower, an active period of construction and participation and then a defined end. The whole installation was promptly removed at the termination of the project, at a precisely specified time. It was this removal and loss of something that residents saw they had built up themselves, against all the odds, and which quickly had became a positive part of their lives, that spurred them into a realisation of what it was possible to do themselves.

Vertical Living made clear to me that there is a continuous and fundamental process by which we all layer ourselves on to a background environment. This layering is especially pertinent when reality is perceived as institutional and anonymous, and is made as part of a process in order to claim it for the self. Consequently, the layering process became a pivotal point in my working relationship with people and buildings, with the outcome leading me to explore diverse buildings and contexts.

Feelings of alienation and hostility from residents, against the occupation of tower and slab blocks have certainly built up since the beginning of the 1980s when the community value structures underpinning modernist building became officially stigmatised, coupled

with the rise in the ideology of possession and individual enterprise. From my personal experience, whether residents feel hostility and alienation seems to vary from building to building, for in some, people are negative, and in others positive. This was brought home to me very poignantly when working in Leeds on an installation

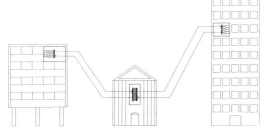

which was to be situated in three buildings, the City Art Gallery, and two nearby tower blocks[6] (*below and left*).

The tower blocks were of exactly the same design, built at the same time, situated near each other, with the residents initially coming from the same redeveloped part of Leeds. Marlborough Towers was an example of how life in the tower block was meant to be, expressing community values, while the other, Lovell Park Towers, represented the worst nightmare of those allocated a flat in one of these buildings. In Marlborough Towers, residents had positioned plants outside the front doors, had personalised knockers and doorknobs, welcoming mats and the place was spotless. By contrast, Lovell Park Towers was devoid of anything similar, it was dark and decrepit, with steel doors and grills erected by some tenants to keep others out of their flats, flats in which they felt imprisoned. When I looked for an answer to this phenomenon, I found that both buildings had started in the same manner, but then one had been allocated 'short-term' problem families as tenants. Their aggressive behaviour towards the situation had triggered off a stigma which blackened residents' feelings about the building. This had developed into a continuous negative feedback, which left people with a psychology that only re-emphasised the full extent of the blight.

In contrast to the external and projected stigmatisation of the tower block and slab block, residents can become engaged in a continual reconstruction of their living space. This can ensure a feeling that the home environment maintains a currency with contemporary culture. At Harvey House in Brentford, West London, where I made *Brentford Towers* in 1985, it was noticeable that many of the residents I worked with had consciously remade the interior of their flat environment, perhaps several times. This had resulted in objects being acquired for their referential ties to an ambience of what at various times they had thought constituted contemporary culture. This also widened the psychology and topology of the space to embrace the cultural world outside with which the person felt they were in touch. If the language of those objects and their setting in the living space was perceived as 'contemporary', they also had to exist with objects that definitely denoted past moments in the possessor's life: dissonance enabled them to be separate but coexist. Interestingly, in this environment I found that any reference to the role of art was linked to the re-creation of past moments, and denoted the cultural orientation of the possessor. In this sense the notion of what was considered to be art included items such as models, framed photographs, pennants or flags. A transformation was created by the possessor in the inherent meaning of what constituted an artwork, an act which accompanied many of the objects, a cognitive act, a projection on to the object while its intended function could remain dormant or even denied.

Some objects are much more permanently located than others, and while some denote the psychological desire for immortality, others indicate a feeling of accepting the idea of transience in daily life. While some objects act as a focal point around which behaviour within the living space is dedicated – such as the television – other objects are displaced into the peripherals of perception of the room, and rather like the material fabric of the building, act as a general reinforcement. There is also a strong projection into the private living space of objects that reflect the product diversity so extant in contemporary consumer culture. Here while there appears to be variety and individuality, the underlying function of the object remains universally the same.

When engaged in the making of *Vertical Living* and *Brentford Towers*, the display of iconographic objects was in this mode. However, another classification of objects as agents of exchange was used by residents to create casual and formal interpersonal networks to overcome the isolating structure of the building. At Skeffington Court, whilst making *Vertical Living*, I came across an elderly lady who had taken it upon herself to look after people's milk delivery, collecting empty bottles and making sure correct orders were delivered. This was a means of creating social contact and here the object of attention was creating a means of social exchange. At Harvey House, equivalent objects that created contact were a keep-fit bicycle, children's toys and a budgerigar, which were incidental but fundamental appendages to enlarging the social domain beyond the flat environment.

It was this transformation that I saw as the real basic creative act from one thing into another. The representation of this creative act within a symbolic world that had strong personal ramifications for the viewer was the primary rationale behind its development. The outcome was that people could make parallel inferences and transformations in their own world. A passive, purely cognitive transformation left the object fixed in place, but a transformation of its behaviour and function often required a symbolic journey to enable the object to move from one state to another: the object then became the catalyst for the possessor to travel between widely differing contexts. This journey is epitomised in the relationship between the housing estate, and adjacent wasteland. Within the rigid determinism of the environment of the housing estate, discarded areas of land take on enormous symbolic functions as an agency. They become a context for activities tangential to the normative environment associated with the estate, but which embody the symbolism for social community.

The process of community activity is triggered by objects transported from the context of ordered determinism (*above right*), institutional society to the entropic anarchy and freedom of nature in the wasteland. The object being taken from context to context is in the process transformed. This metamorphosis formed the parameters to *Pat Purdy and the Glue-Sniffers' Camp*[7] which centred on such a journey as an expression of self-organisation.

The representation of the wasteland as a mythological realm was constructed by the residents living adjacent to it. I understood that they were creating their own symbolic world, in which they could express self-organisation in a way that was impossible within the limiting environment of the housing estate. The construction of special languages and codes to accompany these activities and the externalisation of their alienation from the

norms and conventions of society was a key agent in keeping that society at bay, and in so doing bound the group together. In this journey the can of glue became an icon for the group associated with society, where it had a positive function of sticking things together, to the wasteland where it became the catalyst for expressing an anarchistic freedom. In effect these icons were transported not only physically but went through huge mental journeys between alien psychological worlds.

During the time I spent with Pat Purdy on the Avondale Estate, over a nine month period in 1980, I made several walks with her into the adjacent wasteland which was know locally as The Lurky Place,[8] to a particular camp site she had helped create. I noticed the importance of the wire fence that supposedly separated the estate from the wasteland. It formed a symbolic divider between realities, a point of change in the passage from one psychological realm to another. The small hole in the fence, the activity of having to squeeze through, signified birth and rebirth into the opposite realm. The fence itself was the catalyst for the moment of transformation and at the same time represented the channel for transportation.

The transformation of objects and accompanying perceptual transformations take place in all kinds of environmental circumstances as a means of subverting normality. I have documented many such situations with one thing in common: they occur within a contained and determined space. This is especially the case when I have been engaged with people in working environments where the process of work has given a person a very restricted and deterministic physical and psychological realm to operate within.[9] One working environment in which I focused a series of works was the modern office, and in particular the space that immediately confronts every office worker – the office desk. This space, one in which office workers sit for vast amounts of their life, was seen as a territory that was both institutional and personal, a private realm within the structure of the open, more public structure of the building. In the desk space, objects are brought together into a coexistence that represents value structures, and attendant perceptual realms that are in permanent opposition. There is a struggle which is fundamental to the survival of the person sitting there: on the one hand there are objects associated with the determinism of work and which express those values, and on the other there are objects that have been transported into that space to express something about the identity and psychology of the person behind the desk. In the installations I made from my involvement with people working in the very modern office buildings of Merrill Lynch in New York, and Swann House in Newcastle, I noted that objects were also purposefully transported into the building to enlarge the psychological realm of the person sitting at the desk; to exhibit variety within the highly reductive environment of the building. However, such expressions of a person's self-organisation had to take place within a sphere of what was permissible, and providing that the transportations were made inside what was known to be tolerated, complex and bold articulations could be made without damaging work prospects, in fact it could even enhance them. The representation of the world beyond the interior world of the building, the immediate space in front of the person, specifically triggered mental journeys away from that space into the past, present and future. In so doing, the domain in which the person existed increased, so the space and surface of the desk on which the objects were positioned became an agent, the equivalent of a symbolic window, a divider between realities.

I was similarly aware, in the development of my work at Harvey House and all other tower and slab blocks that I have encountered, of the major subconscious role of the living room window. It is a means of encoding the external world enabling projections to be made on to it that manifest the transformation of reality by the residents. Thus residents created a world they could see, but not touch, and from which they were effectively distanced. In *Brentford Towers* I incorporated this act of transformation into the making of the work by asking residents participating in the symbolic group to make a connection between an object in their living room, and an object they could see in the landscape from the living room window, and then to describe the relationship.

This was done in the same manner with Pat Purdy where I asked her to make a relationship between the contexts of the wasteland and the estate, and the objects transported in the journey between them. This she did effectively by taking the idea a stage further and suggesting that the actual objects I was photographing be incorporated into the work. Pat Purdy's act of developing the form of the work, I see as typifying my relationship with the people I work with – a relationship which I see as an expression of mutuality, the interactive interpersonal paradigm that underlies my conception of self-organisation.

I consider that the methodology involved in making a work is in itself an expression of the same message, one that underpins the reception of the work in whatever environment, whether in an art museum, housing complex or office block. It presents the message and ensures that the relationship between conception and reception is consistent (*below*). Thus, while I see buildings as an institutional expression, I see the installations within buildings presented here as an expression of the counter-consciousness of a community.

Notes

1 This formative work took place in two districts of Nottingham in 1970 with a group of students from the Department of Fine Art, Trent Polytechnic. It is discussed in: *Control* Magazine No. 6 1972; Stephen Willats, *Art and Social Function*, Latimer New Dimensions (London) 1976; Willats, *The Artist as an Instigator of Changes in Social Cognition and Behaviour*, Gallery House Press (London) 1973.

2 *The Social Resource Project For Tennis Clubs* (1971) was a conceptual and dynamic process of events that were structured over several months and engaged members of four tennis clubs in Nottingham in remodelling the game of tennis around their real needs for club membership. A tournament was played under the new rules. The work is discussed by Martin Kunz in 'Rationale englische Kunst-tendenzen', *Kunst Nachrichten*, Heft 7 (Basel) March 1973. Also in *Art and Social Function*; *The Artist as an Instigator of Changes in Social Cognition and Behaviour*.

3 *Art and Social Function*; 'West London Social Resource Project', *Studio International*, Vol 185, No. 951; 'Constructing Operational Models Of Art Practice', *Control* Magazine, No. 7, 1973; 'Art And Social Function: Prescriptions', *Art and Artists*, Vol 8, No. 87.

4 In the development of my approach towards contextualising language I was influenced by the work of Basil Bernstein who published extensively in the 1960s. Bernstein defines two basic types of codes, 'elaborated' and 'restricted', which in his paper, 'Linguistic Codes, Hesitation Phenomena and Intelligence', are referred to in a linguistic context. However, similar parallels can be made with a visual one: 'Two general types of code can be distinguished: Elaborated and Restricted. They can be defined, on a linguistic level, in terms of the probability of predicting for any one speaker which structured elements will be used to organise meaning. In the case of an elaborated code, the speaker will select from a relatively extensive range of alternatives and therefore the probability of predicting the pattern of organising elements is considerably reduced. In the case of a restricted code the number of these alternatives is severely limited, and the probability of predicting the pattern is greatly increased.' Another reference is Bernstein, 'Social Structure, Language and Learning' *Education Research*, 3, 1963.

5 A detailed analysis of the concepts and methodologies involved in the development and presentation of *Vertical Living* is made in Willats, 'The Counter-Consciousness in Vertical Living', *Control* Magazine No. 11, 1979. An archive with original material related to the work is kept in the archives at the Tate Gallery, London.

6 The installation *From Different Worlds* (Leeds) 1987, involved people making a walk between three separate buildings in order to experience the complete work. A model of this installation is presented in the accompanying catalogue *Between Objects and People* (Leeds City Art Gallery) 1987.

7 There have been many published discussions about *Pat Purdy and the Glue-Sniffers' Camp*, though I refer the reader to the text by Stephen Bann, 'A Hole in the Wire', in the catalogue *The Boundary Rider*, 9th Biennale of Sydney, 1993.

8 The wasteland area formed the context for a number of works made before I met Pat Purdy, one of which took the form of a bookwork *The Lurky Place*, Lisson Gallery (London) 1978.

9 *Transformers*, Laing Art Gallery (Newcastle) 1988. Gray Watson, 'Beyond Determinism', in the catalogue *Secret Language*, Corner House (Manchester) 1989. See also the writings in Willats, *Intervention and Audience*, Coracle Press (London) 1986.

Captions
PAGE 6: One of a series of three art and society self-published manifestos, Stephen Willats, 1961.
PAGE 7: Organic Exercise No. 6, *Series Two, tower block study, 1962, 50.8cm wide by 63.5cm high. Ink on paper, private collection, Paris.*
PAGE 8: A basic model for a homeostatic self-organising system, showing total coupling between elements A, B, C, D. From Life Codes and Behaviour Parameters, *The Midland Group (Nottingham) 1976.*
PAGE 9: Social Resource Project for Tennis Clubs, *1971.*
PAGE 10: West London Social Resource Project, *1972-73: flow chart of events during the nine months of the project; project area leaflets; public register board* in situ.
PAGE 13: Conceptual Tower, 1977.
PAGE 14: Vertical Living, *one of the seven display boards.*
PAGE 16: From Different Worlds, Elevated Objects, *1987, the installation at Marlborough Towers.*
PAGE 17: A Work Involving Three Culturally Separated Institutions, *1987.*
PAGE 19: The Lurky Place, the wasteland adjacent to the Avondale Estate.
PAGE 20: Problem display boards from Contained Living, *1978.*

The Emergence of a New Reality

It is a significant factor in contemporary living that during the last fifty years our conceptions of, and expectations from, the everyday world have become more predetermined and at the same time more complex. A social and physical 'new reality' has emerged that is authoritatively shaped and controlled by 'institutions', and which is specifically a product of planning how people should live in an urban society that is to be kept stable within the norms and priorities of a higher authority that has been vested in institutions. Right from the start, there is an obvious basic division between the minority who determine the topology of urban living, and the majority who are forced to passively accept its form in their daily lives.[1]

It is the reality in which people live and work that is the most important to them. So it is in these areas that our culture overtly expresses the ideological consciousness upon which it is founded. What is recognised in the planning of the new reality is the very strong connection between the way in which a person forms their social consciousness and the physical environment in which they live and work. Increasingly, the topology of the everyday world has come under the influence of the professional, the architect, the planner and the social worker, and thus reflects their own norms and values and aspirations. Integral to the concept of the new reality is that it is new and planned – a better way of living for large numbers of people. It is therefore important for the professional in his conceptions to create a separation from the past or from ways of life that run counter to the norms and conventions of the dominant culture. The career pressures on the professional to create such a separation are considerable and have led to the 'newness' of the new reality being constantly proclaimed, it has also led to a self-referenced, uniform and bleak repetitiveness in the physical form that it has been given.

Institutions

Established by society to ensure that the physical environment and people's social behaviour remain under its determining influence, institutions manifest themselves in a wide variety of ways. They range from planning departments of the municipal authorities, to community centres, schools, newspapers and television. In fact, one view of contemporary society is that it is comprised of a network of interlinked institutions, all of which agency various areas of control over people. Thus the explicit function in the establishing of institutions is generally to preserve the *status quo* as determined by the possessors of decision-making power.[2] The influence of these institutions in shaping the physical world of the new reality lies within four broad areas:

- Maintenance and preservation.

- Enforcing norms and codes of behaviour.
- Providing a point of reference.
- Providing idealised symbols for people to emulate.

These institutions present themselves and are legitimised by the rest of society as vested with expert knowledge; this authority is reinforced by the distance created between themselves and the people their decisions will affect.

The World of Objects

The ownership of property forms a parameter to the fabric of Western society, its acquisition and maintenance underlying the structure of values from which the culture derives. The power given to property is symbolised through the possession of objects, especially those objects that can reinforce the idealisations projected through society's fabric of institutions. A constant pressure is exerted on the consciousness of the individual generated by specially constituted institutions, that is, advertising agencies, broadcasting corporations and newspaper empires, to view the world as one comprised of objects.[3] More specifically, a world of those objects that have been created and approved, because of the deterministic influences associated with their acquisition and use. This pressure exerted through media constraints, such as women's magazines, television and bill boards, is so great that not only are other people perceived as objects, but the self also.

The desiring of objects often leads people away from involvement in any meaningful relationship with the community. In modern life there is a two-way neutralising pull on the individual consciousness: one is the basic drive to conform to group norms implicitly held by any functioning community; the other to reduce the values of human involvement beneath that of the desire to possess objects. The latter pull is enormously strong, for the associative behaviours and attitudes given to the possession of objects psychologically provides and replaces the norms and values that are deficient because of a lack of community involvement. Community attitudes and values may conflict with the surrounding institutional structure, while those the individual acquires through attending to the possession of objects are more easily predetermined by the institutions that generated those objects in the first place. It is thus an important priority of those institutions that a person perceives himself as wanting to live within a world comprised of objects, the objects of implied power.

Separation From Nature

The exercise of control over the so-called 'natural environment' in order to survive is a fundamental task of any society. In the new reality this control is continually impressed on the consciousness of people through the encoding of the physical environment into a highly complex structure of interrelated symbols that exhibit their separation from nature. This control is greatly emphasised by stating a high degree of technological achievement in the formation of rigid structures into slab blocks and towers, and by creating a highly defined boundary around them. These developments are not just removed from nature but are separated by their defined boundaries from other urban developments nearby. Thus a housing estate or office block complex exists in the professional's conception as contained islands, and this is given an added symbolic meaning by delineating a boundary between the internal state's order and the disorder of external nature. Nature is the symbol of the 'counter-force' of entropy, untamed and always moving towards anarchy, and as a threat to the stability of the infrastructure of society, it is therefore repressed.

While nature is repressed, certain natural elements are included in the plans of the new reality, but only as a demonstration of how they can be held within a fixed framework, again impressing on the inhabitants' psychology the degree to which they are living within a predetermined environment. Through the professional, society appropriates 'nature', and encodes it into its own system of beliefs and values, neutralising what is considered to be its disruptive potential and instead displaying isolated elements that are held as its own cultural products. Of special symbolic significance are the wasteland boundaries between the order of the new reality and the inferred wilderness of surrounding nature. These not only exist between urban developments, but within them, where they take on a special meaning as discarded remnants that again constantly remind the new reality's inhabitants of their own separation from nature.

The encoding process into symbols of order is achieved through a combination of media and form, such as in the use of concrete, aluminium or glass in the reduction of a building into angular, square and repetitive monumental shapes. All this constantly impresses on the individual consciousness that someone else is exercising control on his behalf over the natural elements that could otherwise disrupt the determinism of the world in which they live.

The Provision of Resources

Integral to the idea of society is that resources are provided which can be used by the community and the individual to facilitate their own social well-being. These social resources are either set up by the official institutional mechanisms of society, or more importantly are established by the community themselves. In this sense they are officially part of the plan for the new reality or unofficial, not approved or envisaged in the plan.

Within a person's everyday experiences, social resources exist in an interdependent triangular relationship with domestic and economic realities, and are the vehicle for social exchange and the establishing of attitudes. They come in many different guises, and are not necessarily housed in a special building, such as a community hall. They can be associated with a behavioural routine; for example, contact created between residents while visiting a particular local shop. Other social resources, though they may be associated with a particular task for the individual such as eating or exercise, have the more general function of maintaining the social cohesiveness and stability of the community. Certainly, as the planners of the new reality have discovered, when official resources such as restaurants, playgrounds and community centres, are not present in their plans, then the fabric of the community begins to break down, or simply does not exist.

Unofficial social resources are generated by the community trapped in the new reality because of the lack of official provision, or because of the professional authorities' inability to represent community priorities and feelings. Also, people have no wish to be contained within officially determined boundaries, and when they become aware of them they react strongly against them, creating their own resources as agents to move outside what has been prescribed. These resources are much more diverse than the official ones, and can, comprise, for example, a wall used for graffiti or a piece of wasteland associated with values and behaviours that are outside planned urban life. They are an escape from the pressures of living and working within the contained conditions of the new reality and are also a manifestation of a counter-consciousness of social contact and community involvement that implicitly responds to the complexity in the psychological make-up of individuals.

Living Space as Institutions

The domestic interior living space has become an important agent for our culture in symbolising its idealisations. It is the primary context for the ideological foundations of the dominant culture to be constantly stated to the individual and thus, ultimately, to the community. The living space is encoded into an ideal type that is then projected through the media to the individual. By shaping the domestic space in accordance with projected ideal types, an ideology can be ever-present, and like everything else in the new reality, what occurs can be under the constant shadow of society's institutions. The basic constructs in our consciousness of ourselves and others are moulded by that part of the environment in which we want to be most free and expressive. The physicality and inflexibility of the living space's structural mass means that it is the inhabitants who must adapt as soon as they move in. This feeling of restriction and passivity is strengthened by the rules and regulations that accompany the life within its confines. For the interiors of the housing blocks do not adapt themselves to the inhabitants' requirements; they cannot influence the planner of their own living spaces, they can only modify its surfaces and position objects within it to state their own identities and values.

While the layout and position of the housing block have been predetermined, so has the content, but in a different, more subtle way. For the media also projects 'models' of preferred ways of life that are there simply to be emulated. The media's representations of the 'model' bring together various objects that denote forms of success, power and ability, and these are expressed to people as desirable attributes; ones they should have themselves.[4] The inference is that a person will acquire these attributes by making similar arrangements with objects in their own homes.

Hidden Tensions, Frustrations and Anger

Despite the hard, grey, cold exterior of the new reality's concrete blocks, human emotions still exist, though only as a hidden element that is revealed to the outside world through the drawings and slogans on the walls of buildings, in the corridors and generally through evidence of vandalism. Small informal networks of relationships, between neighbours, parents or within family groups, generate reactions to the environment, but in the absence of any means of public expression they are bottled up, compressed into small interpersonal structures that gnaw away at the inner self. Tension is fuelled by stories generated via neighbours, casual acquaintances met in lifts and elsewhere, of muggings, break-ins, police activity, sex parties and so on. This has produced an uneasiness of outlook, reinforced not surprisingly by the lack of jobs, little money and the continual fate of being trapped forever in a concrete block. In the end this gets into people to such an extent that it creates a sense of their own uselessness and ineffectuality. Consequently, people are turning on what is nearest to them, what is ever-present and a reminder of the state they are in, the concrete blocks themselves are coming under attack, the block they are living in, their own domestic world. They quite simply just want to smash it up, and get out. However, since there is no possibility of social or economic mobility, and with no means of articulating their own feelings in the open, a general emotional state, initially of repression and then anger, is building within the grey concrete walls of the blocks.

The State of No Culture

One recent important, though negative, development in the daily lives of people in the housing projects of the new reality has been the demise of their ability to generate their own culture. Traditional working-class communities have long been associated with the making of their own special culture, which has been completely displaced in their occupancy of the new reality. While it is not always the case, people coming into a new housing project are drawn from no specific community: their arrival relates to their individual circumstances rather than that of a whole community. In time a new community might well be expected to form to combat the initial displacement of residents and this would eventually generate its own forms of culture. But the rapid turnover of residents, their drive to get out as fast as they can, and the segmented physical environment itself, constantly prevent this.

From the section of the community with the most energy – the young – spontaneous outbursts of creativity do break through the surrounding restrictive environment. The strongest form that this creative energy takes is in music, usually initially created by messing about in parents' living rooms. Punk culture was the strongest articulated response to the new reality: its motivation and form directly stemmed from the repressiveness of the environment. Punk music and clothes were an overt expression to the world outside of the kids' alienation and their determination to fight back. Other equally important manifestations were the fanzines and different forms of dancing such as the 'pogo'. The importance of punk culture was in its contextualisation; initially it came directly from the context to which it addressed itself, and was an aggressive confrontation with the notion of professionalism. You too could be a 'mini star', as an individual on your own housing estate. The whole basis of DIY in punk culture was a manifestation of self-organisation. Punk culture was temporary, transitory and thus largely as anonymous as the grey concrete slabs of the new reality. However, it has gone the way of all other forms of resistance to the institutional fabric and been subverted, through being institutionalised, thus giving way to a state of no culture, for nothing has regenerated itself to replace it. Kids are again presented with idealisations to worship as a diversion from the crumbling fabric of the new reality immediately around them. The state of no culture is the current state of culture.

Two Consciousnesses in Opposition

An object-based consciousness predominates in our culture: that of society's institutions. A person-based consciousness, that of the community, has to exist as a counter-consciousness because it is considered subversive to a controlled predetermined social fabric. The full social and psychological complexity of people is recognised in counter-consciousness which is built around a mutual involvement between people. Implicit in this is the downgrading of the social priority to possess property. Counter-consciousness is self-organising; relationships between people are self-determined and formed from what they can mutually ascertain are their priorities and needs. Thus all persons are more directly involved in establishing their own community – the one in which they live – participating in the decisions that affect their daily life.

The Creation of a Parallel World

The fundamental fight against surrounding determinism is of vital importance to the people living within the new reality. People simply do not want to give in, and despite the enormous psychological and physical pressures on them to be passive, there is a continual struggle to establish their own individual identity and retain contact with other people living in the same area.[5] Here, counter-consciousness exists as a kind of underground network within the new reality and is a parallel world that is in an enforced coexistence with its surroundings.

Even without any real organisation such as a tenants' association, residents try to forge their own network or relationships with other residents, even if it is just with their immediate neighbours. The odds must be counted as definitely against people, but even so, another world can be built (even if only symbolically) that still shows there is the will to establish a different social consciousness of community-based values.

Landings and lifts form points of contact within the boundaries of the new reality, and these become important contexts for establishing a counter-consciousness. It only requires one or two articulate people to create a coherent picture of the environment, and motivation to react against their condition, for there to be the potential for establishing organised and meaningful communication. However, the totality of isolating pressures in the new reality and the interlinking between media and physical actuality, make the construction of a coherent total view extremely difficult. Generally, people's perceptual models of the surroundings in which they live are highly fragmented and contextual, built on just their own immediate experience.[6] Such fragmentary impressions, reactions and tensions significantly contribute to people's inability to act for themselves. However, there is the chance for people to extend the boundaries of their contained lives by creating new territories of activity, thus making an active context for the creation of a parallel world. The alienation of the territory must be important to the manifestation of such activities that are in themselves alienated from the dominant culture the people are trying to escape from. Alienation is a crucial key to building an identity for those people who go to the created territory; common hatred of the new reality is the catalyst for the formation of a larger community feeling that can be transferred back into everyday life within the confines of the housing estate.

Reactions to Pressure

Reactions by residents against the constant pressures of the new reality are largely set up in response to a totality that is perceived as all-embracing, cold, and authoritative. It creates the rules and at the same time is removed and amorphous. 'Who do we deal with? The world seems full of faceless professional bureaucrats.' Against this kind of reaction, people's responses seem to fall into a number of categories, all of which can be associated in some way with the notion of counter-consciousness. Perhaps the most overt response is where people seek to destroy the environment in which they are trapped, by either directly vandalising it, or (depending on your viewpoint) breaking it up by misusing or re-using the provided facilities. The smashing of windows, urinating in lifts and the general destruction of the environment are obvious expressions of resident's anger at being trapped there. Approximately nine months after moving into their flat, a tolerance level is often reached where a resident begins to realise their own isolation, and becomes aware of the existing pressures. This is when the initial euphoria of the flat's newness has worn off, and tensions gradually wind up to a point when people just want to take apart what they can immediately see, as the causing of their anguish.

At another, more subtle level the destruction of the environment is not destruction at all, but is creative; people are simply registering their mark to show that they exist. Acts of so-called vandalism as counter-consciousness are no more than anarchistic exhibitions of people's energies and individualism. Acts of destruction are also symbolic agents to the establishing of a counter-consciousness. For the group activities from which they arise, such as hanging around on stairways, destroying playground facilities, are rarely carried out by a lone person, but are the results of a small group or gang.

On the other hand, formal organisations that register people's reactions to the pressures of the new reality, such as tenants' associations, while they might be the most obvious articulate response, are not necessarily the most effective. In fact while an association must generate some cohesion by its existence, and is an important agent in combating passivity, it is still not capable of fundamentally changing the physicality of people's situation. The important effect of such an organisation is social and internal between actively contributing residents, though for those not directly participating it can put the lid on a situation by seeming to cover up a potential opening for their expression.

Contexts for Manifesting Counter-Consciousness

The unofficial nature of the contexts established to express counter-consciousness is essential to their power as an agent, but equally important is their close relationship to the normal daily behaviours of residents. While wastelands adjacent to or within the new reality are a powerful context to identify with, its real significance lies in how they are used to bring about specific activities, as diverse as track bike riding or glue sniffing. Camp building is one example of how the wasteland is used as an agent for counter-consciousness. Small camps are constructed, comprising just a few car seats, but they can be quite elaborate, involving covered dugouts or structures that may even have a roof made of something like corrugated iron sheeting. The camp has many functions, two of which form a focus for group activities, and providing a screen from the prying eyes of the surrounding urban world. Within the camp, the group or gang is safe to indulge in its own activities, create its own special languages and behaviour. Thus, the more inaccessible and hidden they are from the gaze of outsiders, the better. Pathways and open spaces become the contexts for track bike riding, or horse riding, and while these are individualistic pursuits, and often competitive, they still essentially rely on a group albeit an *ad hoc* one, for support.

Other locations are used to furtively hide, usually those parts of the new reality that are the most screened: stairways, lift landings, the complex of sheds provided for residents' storage and garages, especially those ones that have been abandoned, which always seem to have everyone's rubbish thrown in them. Interestingly, garages should be the one piece of private space that would have the potential to be a vehicle for creativity and communication; however, they are of course separated from the actual blocks where people live and are nearly always without any electricity or water; the basic ingredients for anything to be really created. Instead they are abandoned or broken into.

On the other hand where resistance has been more formally organised by residents through tenants' associations, their own flats are often used and this perhaps represents symbolically the most powerful context of all for manifesting counter-consciousness. In the absence of any provided meeting place in a tower block, Skeffington Court at Hayes, West London, where I made *Living With Practical Realities*[7] and the project *Vertical Living*,[8] the hallway at the front entrance to the tower was initially used. When this became extremely inconvenient, the residents started to open their own flats up on an *ad hoc* basis to the tenants' association for their meetings, though if any administrative work needed doing, then it was always done in one particular resident's living room.

The Transportation of Objects

Objects are important agents in the expression of counter-consciousness, however, in nearly all instances their role is changed from the one given or assigned to them by the dominant authoritative culture from which they originate.[9] The dominant culture's ownership of the means of production, requires that an object's use is either transformed from the one intended, or is extended into a territory in which counter-consciousness can be manifested.

Here the object becomes an agent, as it is the means through which relationships are initiated and enabled within the group, or fantasy roles constructed by the individual; for example, the walker in the wasteland with his air rifle and dog sees himself as the lone hunter in the forest, or some backwoodsman figure.

Instead of an object symbolically replacing relationships with other people as in the dominant cultural consciousness, it is the means through which its pressures can be resisted. Objects become more tool-like, they are the trigger for exchanges between people, and their references by this implication extend into the community: if they do not inherently have this characteristic already, they are given it through their transformation.

One particularly interesting transformation is the can of glue. In one context it has a deterministic, constructional role; the making and repairing of objects. This is its positivistic role within the dominant culture, but is completely negated by young people who transform this by sniffing the glue to get high. Even more significant is the taking of the glue can into a wasteland where it is the prime agent for the building of a camp, an important context for generating group cohesiveness. The crucial factor is that the very alienation of glue sniffing as an activity amongst young people from the dominant cultural norms is crucial to its functioning as their means of escape. Ultimately, the most important form of glue-sniffing is communal, where the can is burnt on a fire that forms the centre point of the camp, as this then involves the transformation of other objects as part of the resulting anarchistic group high. Cars are driven into the wasteland and set alight, then left as rusting monuments to the group's activities, eventually to be supplanted by the forces of wilderness and to find a harmony with them. This again is a specific transportation of an object from one context to the other, also small objects that are already scattered around, or have been brought over to the camp by the group are picked up and utilised, often with extreme points of energy. The can of glue is a highly symbolic object in this context because from its transformation other objects are also transformed to act as agents for counter-consciousness. There are many other alien activities that involve transformation, for example, on the Avondale Estate in Hayes, West London, tenants stood on the bath in their flat so that they could place an ear against the air vent outlet, and from this everyone's conversations in the whole block could be heard, thus transforming air vent to receiver.

This is an edited extract from The New Reality, *1982.*

Notes

1 These ideas are extensively explored in an essay published in Stephen Willats, *Living Within Contained Conditions*, MOMA (Oxford) 1978, and then later in the exhibition catalogue *Leben in Vorgegbenen Grenzen – 4 Inseln in Berlin*, Nationalgalerie Berlin, 1980-81; *Marxism and the Metropolis*, ed Wiliam K Tabb and Larry Sawers, Oxford University Press, 1978, for a very pertinent exposition on contemporary urban issues as affecting the 'new reality' of American cities.

2 Stafford Beer, *Decision And Control*, John Wiley & Sons (Chichester) 1966, presents an interesting critique of existing decision-making control mechanisms in society.

3 The relationship between different social consciousness and the perception of people and self as objects is presented in a paper by Dale Lake which I found particularly pertinent to my own thinking. The paper is titled *Perceiving And Behaving*, Teachers' College Press (New York) 1970. Also influential to my thinking were the studies presented in *Topics Of Social Psychology*, ed Charles Kiesler, Addison-Wesley Publishing Company, London. Particularly important to me were Kiesler and Kiesler, *Conformity*, Addison-Wesley Publishing Company, 1970, and *Group Performance*, Jones Davis, 1969.

4 Varda Langholz Leymore, *Hidden Myth (Structure and Symbolism in Advertising)*, Heinemann (London) 1975.

5 I think a fascinating booklet was published by the tenants of the Honor Oak Estate, about how they saw their history and current everyday life there. The booklet represents the tenants' fight against the anonymity of their surroundings: *A Street Door of Our Own*, Honor Oak Neighbourhood Association, London SE4.

6 Basil Bernstein has based his considerable influential theories on the contextualisation of language and thought patterns, what he calls 'Restricted Codes' and 'Restricted Thought Process'. A good critique to Bernstein's theories is made by Harold Rosen, and his discussion is also relevant to the general assumptions made by the 'professional' about the residents of municipal housing schemes: Harold Rosen, *Language and Class*, Falling Wall Press (Bristol) 1972.

7 This work is fully reproduced and discussed in *Living Within Contained Conditions*.

8 Stephen Willats, 'The Counter-Consciousness in Vertical Living', *Control* Magazine, No.11, November 1979, p4.

9 'The Lurky Place' is the name given to the large area of wasteland adjacent to the Avondale Estate in Hayes. Although I first came across it in 1972, I didn't start fully exploring it until 1976, and while doing so I was struck by the many functions this piece of discarded land had for the estate residents. I started to photograph objects brought over to the Lurky Place by residents to facilitate their activities there and then discarded. From this documentation I produced my only landscape work, *The Lurky Place*, Lisson Gallery (London) 1978.

An Island Within an Island

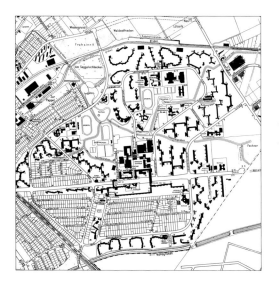

Having arrived in West Berlin in April 1979 to start my DAAD Fellowship, I made a five-day reconnaissance drive during which two contexts I subsequently used to make a work more or less immediately presented themselves. Huge modern housing developments at Märkisches Viertel in North Berlin, and Gropius Stadt in South Berlin were obvious manifestations of an institutional new reality. Both were the result of internationally known architects and planners, brought into Berlin to create these very special environments as obvious status symbols. The following contexts were specified:

- A large block of 350 flats at Märkisches Viertel – *dependency*.
- A residential tower block at Gropius Stadt, South Berlin – *isolation.*

Each work was to come from a co-operation established between myself and an individual or group present in each situation. It was intended that the works, as well as forming an installation within a public art institution, for example, The National Gallery, would also be individually presented in the contexts from which references are drawn. The piece, concerned with isolation and using the context of a tower block in Gropius Stadt, was also presented as an installation in the base of the actual tower, and the work on dependency was set up in the foyer of the flats at Märkisches Viertel.

Thus the works formed a model of practice that involves an interaction between different individuals and groups, as well as institutions operating at different levels within the same 'authoritative culture'.

Dependency: *Wie Ich Entdeche, das wir von Anderen Abhängig Sind*

While the Märkisches Viertel represents the new reality, it is still founded on fundamental social relationships that have become the basis of any society. Large blocks represent the determinism of our own culture, in that they constitute a fixed environment that cannot be adapted or changed by the occupants, but which nevertheless exerts a constant pressure on them to live within the planned constraints. The rules set by the structure also contain the underlying fundamentals to social organisation, this being one person's ability to be able to depend on the service of another. Within the block this dependency on others was epitomised for me by the service of the caretaker to his tenants. The work divides this dependency into three areas of responsibility:

- Maintaining the physical environment.
- Enforcing a code of conduct.
- Providing a point of reference.

Within each area the relationship is viewed firstly in terms of 'problem situations' that exist for the caretaker, and secondly through the response of the tenants, the two fundamental perceptions linked by an intermediary object. While this intermediary object is the agent of exchange in the relationship, it also divides the two perceptual territories that exist.

In the fixed environment of the block of flats, the tenant takes the service of the caretaker for granted, his service is constant until a problem situation arises that disrupts it and sets up a conflict in the dependency. While such relationships of service are the basis of the workings of our society, the service of the caretaker in maintaining the living environment of 350 tenants, within that particular reality of the Märkisches Viertel, is an amplification of our own position.

Isolation: *In Isolation Leben*

Gropius Stadt in South Berlin was developed in the mid-1960s when the tower block was the city planners' favourite solution to seemingly all housing shortages. Not surprisingly, it has proliferated at Gropius Stadt, completely dominating the landscape with white structures that in one particular case reaches twenty-nine stories. This tower forms the context for the work *In Isolation Leben*. The participant in this work was a family man with four grown sons who lived together in a two-room flat at the top of the tower. The internal world of the flat, and the man's position within it – isolated from the outside world both psychologically and physically – forms the work's area of attention. The participant did not accept the fixed nature of his physical surroundings and carried out a number of different DIY schemes to relate the flat more to his family's needs, as well as to values associated with where he lived before in Kreuzberg. Thus the work concerns the relationship between the inducement of separation and passivity by the environment of the tower, and a person's ability to express counter-consciousness through their own actions. Four areas in which the man is isolated are defined in four panels that comprise the piece:

- Psychological isolation from the past.
- Social isolation from the surrounding community.
- Economic isolation from resources.
- Cultural isolation from a means of expression.

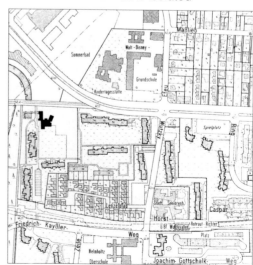

Within each area there exists a problem situation that defines a conflict between the man's life in the tower and each of the four areas of isolation. Objects that exist within the world of the man's flat denote an internal determinism that exercises a pressure on him, and others denote agents for counter-consciousness, for the means of resistance.

Herr and Frau Hoffmann, June 1979

SW *I'm sitting in Märkisches Viertel and I'm speaking to Herr and Frau Hoffmann at Strasse 6. You're the caretaker for number 6 and I wondered if you could tell me in your own words how you see this particular block?*

Frau H We have two opinions on this. My husband has a different opinion to me. Mine is that as I am working I occasionally meet a tenant. He either grumbles or he has worries. Otherwise we have to make sure that everything here is clean and orderly. We have to call the workmen, we also have to make sure that the workmen do their work properly because sometimes we have to deliver reports on this.

Herr H Well, we are caretakers and we have 290 housing units in here. We have to care for and keep clean five blocks. This is our job here.

SW *And your opinion of it? Do you like it?*

Herr H Well, I like, well we have a secure position here, right? The job we do is relatively crisis-secure, and we can . . .

Frau H . . . Work flexible hours as well. Let's say, today we don't have the mind and we want to cease working early, we can do that, and so another day we have to work longer. It doesn't matter as long as we do our job. Every four weeks, however, we are confined to quarters, as I call it. Then we are not allowed to leave home at either day or night. That is, one of us has always to be here – there are altogether forty-four lifts in these houses which have to be looked after – it is possible that we have to run over the field, as we say, for ten minutes to free perhaps someone from the lift if he is stuck between floors, or if there is another problem. By and large, we have coped up to now. But we can't say we stop working at four o'clock, we are always on duty, be it at night, if the tenants have any requests.

Herr H And we ourselves don't have a surgery, the tenants come when they have problems, in the early morning at six or at night at ten, whether it is a leaking tap or the drains are blocked and, 'my husband is ill, what shall I do?' Or the neighbour comes: 'I haven't seen this old gentleman since yesterday and the food which he gets from the Red Cross, is still there, what shall we do?' So we call for the fire brigade. Then the fire brigade arrives and breaks open the door, and the good man isn't there. Afterwards it turned out that he had been to the East at his granddaughter's. Well, these things happen at night, don't they? And therefore we cannot say we have any free time.

SW *About how many people live in the blocks that you care for, and what is the actual composition of the tenants – what kind of people live here?*

Herr H I mentioned this at the beginning, that we have about 288 units here. Living here are workers, staff employees and civil servants, so you could say lower up to middle class, because these are council flats and the people that moved in had to have a certain income, a low one.

SW *In the usual course of your work what kinds of encounters do you have with people?*

Frau H This is easier to answer. Well, first, as I said, our work consists in keeping the blocks clean. It is added – if you have objections, make yourself heard please – that all workmen have to report to us, to fetch the keys for the respective blocks so that they can get in. Then, the workmen have to be called by us, partly via the administration, partly by ourselves. As for the tenants, they sometimes ring us late at night: 'Herr Hoffmann, come, I've forgotten my key, please unlock the door.' And if this doesn't work, we have to call the fire brigade or the locksmith, who is of course very expensive. For the tenants, my husband is, as it were, Jack of all trades. He has to comfort many an old lady when she has lost her key or misplaced it. Then he has to unlock the door and to help her to look for it. He doesn't have to, but it's really readiness to help when they come: 'Can you take me to the hospital quickly', which happened recently. This man had a swollen face, so he drove and took him to the hospital. These are all things which add to our job. Yet the tenants gripe: 'This caretaker, he doesn't do anything'.

Others say, 'Why, there are the children who make it all dirty again'. Everything doesn't always look very rosy, but otherwise our work consists of: firstly, to clean; secondly, Jack of all trades, from unlocking doors to pastoral care, because they come along and tell you: I have this and that illness, I have been in the hospital for so and so long. Others tell you, 'My husband has thrown me out', or the husband comes along and says, 'My wife has run away, what in the world can I do?' Sometimes, it's a burden on our nerves. We've got our own problems, and other people come with theirs.

Herr Hoffmann, October 1979

SW I've come again to talk to Herr Hoffmann, and this is just a series of questions that come from looking at the transcripts of the first tape recording we made. Do you keep a certain distance from the people here?
Herr H From the first we have pinned down that we don't want our flat to be used for an open day, and I think having 280 units here, we couldn't practically do our job anymore if we intercommunicated with all of them on a private level. Yes indeed, and besides, we have told ourselves, 'What if someone comes, have you heard?', you know, chit-chat is blossoming here, and my attitude is 'in one ear, out the other', because if I pass an opinion to someone on someone else, five minutes later the same person runs to the other one and says: 'Have you heard what the caretaker said about you?' Oh good gracious, I rather tell myself: no, I do my work, and you mind your business. This is how it is. We have made that our principle.

SW Is there much sort of official or unofficial contact with caretakers working in other blocks? What kind of contact do they have?
Herr H Well, firstly there is official contact, because we four caretakers form a lift stand-by service, which obviously makes contact just in an official way, but besides we get on quite well with the caretakers here, with the four and with other caretakers. We do have

some private contact, but otherwise it's all quiet here. I mean frictions occur everywhere sometimes. The biggest question is always that the lift service is running smoothly. If this is well, all is well.

SW I just wondered if you could relate some personal experiences you have had with the lift alarm when you have been doing it?
Herr H Lift alarm? I can start with the people who are drunk and come home in the middle of the night and press the alarm to check if someone is here. This is how it starts. This is a nuisance of course because, if someone really is in danger . . . well, then I have time for him. Then there was someone who had a key to the lift and used to open the lift doors, and when you open the lift doors, the lift automatically sticks wherever it is. It was very annoying that this bugger would always hang around in the evenings doing that and people would get stuck and call on us, of course. He used to open it downstairs so people would automatically hold it and march in: 'Why, it's dark, there isn't any lift'. Well, we had to actually lodge a complaint with the police against persons unknown. It's an assault, a premeditated assault, isn't it? If someone falls down, we would be responsible if we didn't report it. There's a lot of annoying examples. Listen, we didn't have these rings around the alarm buttons in the beginning, and people just leaned against them. When they touched it, the alarm went off. They don't realise they're ringing. Well, they say, we were wondering because there's this hoot inside the lift. I believe I demonstrated it to you, didn't I. Didn't I show you how I pressed it and hooted? Well it's making a dreadful noise, the hoot itself, and it is also ringing in our flat. And ever since we have taken pain to get these rings, since then it has never hap- pened, and if it does, it's only a lark. They press it and we answer the alarm and ask: Hello, what's the matter? Oh nothing. But didn't you press the alarm, why? Here? We didn't press the alarm! But we heard the alarm, otherwise if we didn't hear the alarm, we couldn't listen in. Then he starts to be- come insolent: Idiot and so on. Then we

switch off. Why should we talk on and on with people? Of course it's always annoying. If it's during the day, it's not so bad because we're always here, but if it happens at night and you jump out of your bed: quick, what's the matter, and then you get stupid answers.

SW Do you think that there is any way that vandalism could be stopped or inhibited around the block or in the lifts?
Herr H You look at it, children can't reach that high so it must also be adults who for a practical joke, or to deal the caretaker a blow, foul the lifts. To my mind all this is more or less gross misdemeanour of people. As far as I've found out, it's mostly not even people that live in the block but guests who come for a visit – they scratch and scrawl swastikas on the walls and such as that, and to my mind that's all gross misdemeanour. In the beginning I used to be angry. After I had had my first nervous breakdown, I said to myself: 'Lick my . . . If they will have it like that, that's their business'. I do my job, I clean up, and if half an hour later they smutch it again. Then they have to stick it for a couple of days or to clean it up themselves, which they can't. They foul the lift, whether they urinate in it or happen to drop their bottle of schnapps, the splash stays. It doesn't cross their minds to take a scouring cloth and to mop it up. They say: 'Are we not paying rent every Monday?' All these are problems which aren't intended, but happen in high spirits or sometimes also as a result of, I don't know, vandalism. A clique of some youths get together and want to show how strong they are. But as I said, sometimes it still annoys me but nowadays I am so mellow already that I say: 'Man, I do my job, I clean it up, and that's it'. If half an hour later there is junk again and stays there, so what? There are other blocks that need cleaning.

Herr and Frau Teller, September 1979

SW I'm sitting on the eleventh floor with Herr and Frau Teller. I'm interested as to how you came to live in the flat, you know, where you came from before and how you actually came to live here, did you apply for it, did you see it advertised or what?

Herr T Yes, I can tell you that. The flat has forms from the senate, social housing construction and we could with our common income just fill it out. We were just over the border of getting the flat at all, and when we were ready and had received the flat we again had to bring the wage certificate, the wage statement. It was already too much, on it states too much, I said 'When you write on it too much you can be content, then you will get the rent from me, when too little you'll get nothing, then you'll have to throw me out', and thus we moved in. The rent from year to year has been raised and already in nine years it has doubled. At first the flat was empty and we didn't see the flat on this floor at all, we weren't allowed to view the flat but we did it! Went there with a carton of cigarettes and a tape measure and said I want to see the flat. The construction workers were there and it was bare brickwork. I said to my wife with the tape measure, the wall of shelves goes here and the bed comes here and that goes there and the sun shone in here and I said that is our flat, we're taking it and then we signed the contract. The drawing of the flat, the architect's plan, it was so small and at the housing office I said, I'm not an architect, I have turned this thing around three times, I said what am I to do with it and he said, ya that is your flat, I said I have to see it first. He said there isn't anything to see and if you go to the construction site then the average construction worker, the foreman has the right to get the police and throw me out, well with cigarettes and with . . . then we took it and we moved here.

SW *Why did you want to move here?*
Herr T We moved out here so that we would finally from pure financial reasons and that was cut as if I would have moved to west Germany.
Frau T In a strange city . . .
Herr T In a strange city and my wife found it very very isolated as we moved over here and I said to her we have to change our lifestyle to fit this satellite state, this communication

vacuum. We were passionate theatregoers – not so very much now – we would ride to the theatre because of the terrible traffic conditions, two and a half hours, till we got there and back again and that discouraged us. When you think about it, both of us are working shifts and we practically don't see each other for two weeks every month except the weekends. One has to plan that little bit of free time. In the beginning the shopping possibilities the communication possibilities were also very very hard, and it is partly so even today, we have a fantastic shopping centre but we shop in the city.

SW Can you give me your impressions of how things have changed in your life here?
Frau T When we moved out here, it was like *Bonanza*: a wilderness here in the house, there were holes, cables . . .
Herr T Like a construction site. Television didn't work, one and a half years the TV didn't always work, through antenna damage and this and that; it was almost like the Wild West. I came out here with my wife before we moved out here, a year before, I was still living in Wedding and back then to look at this satellite state. I said to my wife, that is a thing between Chicago and Vokisa. I said I wouldn't want to be buried here. There was a big sign, 'Here is the Firm Möbelhübner furniturestore', showing a completely furnished floor.

SW Do you have a lot to do with the people around you?
Herr T Watch over, na. The time is bad, the people are worse and we are not the best either (laughter). We don't want this total anonymity, we know the Mixs but we don't socialise with the Mixs, by us it is so.

SW Going back to the flats, do you think they've worn well over the nine years you've been here?
Herr T There's also a lot of satisfaction and I'm not bothered by disturbances, with loud noises for example if parties are happening, well, over there is so far away, I hear it but it doesn't bother me. Soccer is one complete big disaster, soccer can be compared to

carnival – every goal is honoured by a rocket and I don't know where one gets rockets in the summer. I don't need to turn the TV or radio on; I know when every goal is scored. It's very bad in summer, noise tolerance wise, with the motorbike fans.

SW Most likely everywhere, right?
Herr T But with their heavy machines and such around eleven and you're falling asleep and they rattle away, it isn't so good. Otherwise I can even pinpoint through sound when the stores by us close in the summer, when I sit on the balcony and around two o'clock it becomes quiet I know that the stores are closed. It becomes so quiet up here in one sweep and it is a vacation idyll out here, yes truly. Afterwards we will go on the balcony, you can look across towards the eastern section, it is a vacation idyll out here, we are rarely disturbed by traffic noises and that is so wonderfully nice. I have, outside on the balcony from afternoon, evenings, it is wonderful.

SW If anything goes wrong with the flat, can you mend it yourself or do you get help from the owners?
Herr T It depends in which framework it is, we had some damage in connection with the company and indeed it was torn out and newly renovated. I wasn't very happy about it and for about six months. I made sure I got the name of this man so that I would always talk to him so that the secretary couldn't avert me and after a half a year almost into Christmas, I still had this big hole, then I said to him, 'You know something, we're on such good terms, for Christmas holiday come with your family and then we will eat together and will cover up this hole with a big porno picture'. Otherwise up to now I've had no worthwhile difficulties.

Frau Jacob, July 1979

SW Sitting on the eighth floor at number 6, with Frau Jacob. Can you tell me how you came here, intially, nine years ago?

Frau J My son was just a couple of months old we first of all thought it over: we now need a bigger flat – it doesn't work with one room anymore. We registered at different housing-agencies and they told us we must wait at least one year or pay clearance for the flat which was something like five, six thousand marks, money we naturally didn't have. A year passed, by this time it became a little bit critical with us because my son, every now and then, tipped the bathtub over and that was bad. Well, and then we went back because they had not responded, here to the housing agency and they had said it really should already be that far along. The next day there was a letter – so it must have overlapped – and they told us we should go there. We looked at this flat, the crazy thing was that we had to first ask all around where the flat was, because there weren't any numbers. We looked at it and then we said we will take it immediately, that was it. But in the beginning, well, a month or two months ago from the Nine-pin Club, we were talking about it because some already lived here. I had said to them, I will never move there in the Märkisches Viertel, I had said nope, I can't do that: I have the child and because of it I have the responsibility, it won't work. However, we saw the flat here, we had said that it was all the same, first of all from noon onward was sun, which was important because in the mornings we have a lot to do, next day straight hence, signature down, everything was then settled.

SW Do you have much contact with the people around you?
Frau J Yes, I know a lot of people here, first of all here in this house, I find that very good because all our children just about in the same age group and we mainly meet each other downstairs in the sandbox; one starts a conversation through the children, and when there is bad weather we all collect our children together and all of us here into the house. Through that the contact became stronger, and then we decided once one evening to do a bike tour or to go swimming when the children are in bed, as we all had

the same problems with the children. It developed through that and then also with Nine-pin with people always coming into the group.

SW *Have you ever thought that bringing children up on the eighth floor is a problem?*
Frau J I don't see any problem whatsoever. I don't see any difference if I live on the first floor or here on the eighth; the only problems were while the children were small and couldn't even press the eight button or downstairs on the doorbell. I painted the doorbell red and the button in the lift so that the children knew that that was how far they had to go or there is where they had to press, that was all, they first of all needed the size.

SW *Can you think of any changes that have taken place around you or to yourself?*
Frau J First of all there weren't so many shops, and the bus connections were also not so good. The playgrounds were from the beginning the same, I don't know, everything was pretty much finished. Oh yes the doctors, it has become a bit more now the first year or so we still went to Wedding. You got used to that till you find a good one here whether for the children or for myself. That was actually the only difference; slowly one got used to looking for it here and I noticed that going to the old ones is just too far away, and when you hear of a good one, well . . . at the moment I'm still trying to change things for myself so that I can go here to a doctor and not so very far away.

SW *How do you feel about how people care for the condition of the flats?*
Well I must say first of all I like the parlour, firstly because here in the corner one can walk through here also the children when they should romp around or so. They are not always in the way or bump themselves and then I find back there very good when the children are in bed, they still can go to the toilet without disturbing me. When I have guests here, they bid their goodbyes out there and not back there, the children are then not a part of it, that I find very good. The children's room I find a little bit too small, for one child it is just barely enough. Well the bathroom, on the whole I am so content I say to myself if I had now more corridor I would have to pay for more quadratmeter and that is unused room and so I say I have now made two children rooms and I have sort of my bed in the one room, the bed is rarely used by me anyway since my son . . . and now from other people I have heard quite a lot that they also like it. On the other hand there are some who say they don't like it because it is a passage-room, they don't like it they say that one must always go to the back when they must first go through the parlour and I say to myself who has anything to do back there, when I get guests or company they stay here, they go here, except maybe to the toilet or so. Well I like it.

Andreas Jacob and friends, 8 April 1980

SW *I'm sitting in Frau Jacob's flat talking to her son and some of his friends about the drawings that I have seen around and about these flats. Do you find that there is enough for you to do around here?*

– No. Besides, there's only a slide and a sand pit, nothing for older children anyway.

– I don't like them demolishing all playgrounds either. Over there, they have already demolished quite a few, and in two or three where there were logs, they have taken all of them out. Only stones are lying around now. In another one, there was a huge bridge with a wooden frame. First of all, they've pulled out the poles and vandalised the whole. Only stones are lying around now, almost everywhere there are only stones about.

– Afterwards they cleared the field, none of us like that. Now there are only allotments, and we didn't know anymore what to do because for the older children it was good; they could fly their kites. Now you can't do that anymore, it's all houses here, there isn't a breeze.

– Above all, people always grumble. When we walk on the meadow they grumble the meadow gets spoilt. But dogs piss there.

SW So, what kinds of things do you do then around here, if there is nowhere to play? I mean, what do you play, what do you do?

– Völkerball. Mostly, we play ball. Last time the caretaker grumbled again that we weren't allowed to play here, the old people only complained. When we rollerskate down the slope, it's just the same: an old woman grumbles again. It's very bad here.

– We draw squares and play, and as we said, then comes the caretaker, and when we play on the playgrounds on the climbing frame, perhaps in the afternoon, the old people shout down to us and sometimes get the caretaker.

– On the playgrounds, glass splinters are lying about so you can't throw yourself down.

SW How does it go with the grown-ups around you?

– Sometimes well, but mostly the old people grumble.

– Those on the first floor don't mind their own children playing outside on their own – they have two children, but when we play outside they get the caretaker. And I think this is unjust.

SW What do you think could be done then, for you? How do you think they could have made it so that you could have places to play?

– They should build decent playgrounds so that older children can go there.

– And climbing frames – older children climb on them, and the playgrounds are full of gravel and uneven you often fall. And they should make big playgrounds.

SW Any other ideas?

– They should make a big square where everyone can play what they want to. I guess they don't do that, and the caretaker is always

against it, and when we play at number 2, an old woman grumbles and gets the caretaker. The caretaker comes and grumbles at us, and when we play around number 6, someone else grumbles at us.

– Not only that. Once we played Völkerball on the meadow when someone shouted down at us, and some of us said he would come down with a club and threaten them, and when I rollerskated down the slope, someone tipped a bucket of hot water over me so that we would get lost.

SW Can you tell me something now about the drawings, I mean, I have been very interested in them for a long time. Can you tell me what kind of drawings you did, I mean, for instance?

– Me, drawings? I make drawings of someone like cartoons on the ground or on the wall.

SW Can you tell me why you do these drawings?

– At least nobody grumbles at us making them.

– Because nobody sees us.

– Besides, the tenants don't care at all about the houses and how they look, they piss in the corners or break bottles, and everything stays and the caretaker isn't the best, either.

SW Tell me about a drawing you did, describe it a little.

– I drew a face with long hair from the side, it was to picture Claudia, and I wrote underneath 'Claudia', and they put over pebble dashing so that you wouldn't see it because they were sour about it.

SW And why did you do that?

– Because they had drawn a cartoon of me, so I drew a cartoon of her.

SW Is this almost a kind of game?

– Yes, who can tease the others best.

SW And what drawing did you do?

– Well, a head with a long nose, also from the side, and I like drawing warts on it.

SW But do you always draw faces, do you ever draw anything else?

– Well, we played, and I drew a shopping trolley. But they didn't recognise it.

SW And what sort of game was that?

– Well, someone starts off, and the other has to guess what it is.

SW What happens if you get caught doing these drawings?

– I don't care. We run off and come back later and continue drawing.

SW Would you like to do more drawings? Do you think you should just be able to draw anywhere when you want to?

– Especially with coloured chalk. It looks better. Not this shitty yellow wall and only white on it, or over there where it is black, but with proper colour. Or we should block this thing where all the black stuff comes out to make it clean.

SW Can you recognise each other's drawings, do you know who has done the drawings?

– Sometimes. If someone draws very well, you can tell is was so-and-so. If someone does a crippled drawing and he is very bad . . .

– . . . Then you know straightaway it was you!

– Above all, when something is written underneath. You can recognise it by the writing.

– Many of the drawings always have the same shape: round or eggheaded.

SW *You are all about the same age. Do younger and older children draw as well?*

– You notice that. Smaller children do draw, you can tell from the lift. It's always the same drawings. In the lift it says BT at the same height, or some drawings, they are always at the same height.

– I, too, can draw on the ceiling, nobody would see that it was me.

SW *If you see somebody else's drawing, does it make you do another drawings in a related way?*

– Sometimes. If you see one and it's maybe quite a silly one, you do the same drawing and so it goes on and on.

SW *So more as a reply. But that there is a nice drawing and you wish to carry on with it?*

– Sometimes you cross it out.

SW *So some annoy you and you want to get them off?*

– Yes, for example swastikas. I like them most, I always cross them out. Ta-ta-ta-ta-tum, off it comes.

SW *Okay, but when children come from other buildings, do you let them draw on your block?*

– Actually, we do, but when we draw anywhere over there, they grumble at us: 'You can go somewhere else, you can go to your own block, we don't want you to come altogether'.

– Sometimes when I am somewhere on my very own and there's nobody else, I want to look for someone, then I am ever bored. And sometimes in summer when it is ever so hot and a group stand together, they don't know what to do with themselves.

SW *Do you think it might have to do with the way it is here, I mean, do you think there's any*

area where you wouldn't be bored? What would it look like?

– Well, it starts with drawing during the 'after-dinner quiet'. We all play until half past twelve or one, then people start complaining, so we stop it before the caretaker comes, and so we draw out of boredom.

– And my granny once confided to me secretly, she said she had scrawled the walls and done lots of mischief.

– But in most cases they don't say anything.

– They always say that they were better, even though they made the mistakes as we.

SW *Do you think that the grown-ups under-stand understand why you do the drawings?*

– No: 'Why are you doing that, you can't do that, one has to pay for it all'. They always think of money only.

– They also are quite often reserved since they have had unpleasant experiences with children who were very cheeky to them.

– Once I drew on the wall and then I ran away, and suddenly are a man and a woman standing there, walking along. Suddenly this man beats me on my head, I didn't know at all why he was doing it. He hadn't seen me, because I had come around the corner. Suddenly he beats me on my head. Some adults, when they have had unpleasant experiences or are just in a bad mood and see us in the street having fun, they start grumbling at us.

– But you go on drawing all the same. We don't let ourselves be intimidated.

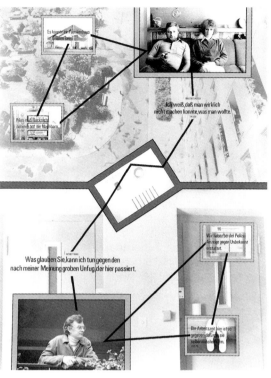

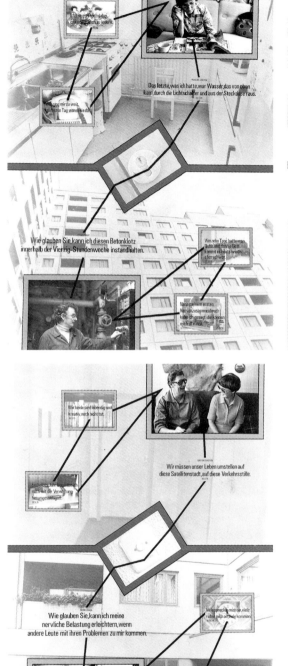

A sequence viewed from above, L to R of Wie ich entdeche, das wir von anderen abhängig sind, *May 1979/March 1980, three panel work, 130cm by 98cm. Photographic prints, photographic dye, Letraset text, ink and gouache, mounted on card*

Von Einer Generation zur Nächsten

Both Frau Jacob and her son, Andreas, who participated in the making of this work, had been involved with me previously when I first visited the Märkisches Viertel in 1978. In going back to work with people I knew before, inevitably it is the intervening time and the accompanying changes that have occurred, that are central. However, I was particularly interested in how their relationship to the immediate environment of their apartment, had evolved, and it is this that has acted as the parameter to the new work.

While the physical fabric of the housing block has remained constant and still radiates its message of modernism, residents' attitudes and perceptions certainly have changed to reflect a different sensibility. Therefore there is a potential conflict between the expression of people's changed attitudes made inside the living environment, and the institutional message on the outface of the building. It is left to the residents to resolve this conflict, and to accommodate, adapt to the building. I feel that what happens is an act of cognitive dissonance by the residents, and that this is symbolic of the present cultural climate; that we are all, in some way, living in the shadow of the unfulfilled promise of modernism.

The work structured between mother and son has been developed from new photographic documentations and tape-recorded interviews, which were later used as the basis of the texts in the work itself. The work centres on two fundamental territories of expression – identity and self-organisation – in relation to the physical mass of the block: objects within the living environment, and signs on the outside of the building. The division of the work into these two territories also parallel the relative perceptions of mother and son.

Frau Jacob, 25 July 1992

SW When I last came it was 1980, twelve years ago. What do you think are the important things that have happened to you in this Wernerheim *in these twelve years?*

Frau J A lot. A lot has changed. I have painted the doors, done the kitchen, made do and mended, purchased new furniture, and in this way a lot has changed. It's no longer all that monochrome.

SW I mean do you think you made a lot of work in here?
Frau J Yes. I've worked a lot in the flat, I've replaced many things so that it's no longer so plain. Before everything was done cheaply so that it wasn't so expensive. New handles on the doors, different coats of paint, I placed handles on the kitchen cupboards so that it looks better than plain flat and white.

SW You seem to have changed the atmosphere in here, the feeling from the white to this. Why?
Frau J I prefer warm tones; everything that's brown, and making everything less severe with a few figurines and such like, so that it isn't quite so sterile, so that you can still live in it and don't have a show flat in which you just live and can't stir. For me it's important that it's cosy and that I can walk about everywhere without having to be particularly careful about breaking or bumping into things.

SW Have you remained in contact with your friends from in the building?
Frau J Yes, I have lots of contact here. I still have friends with whom I go to sport; we have parties together on our birthdays, here or there, or with our neighbours. When our neighbours are on holiday, we water the flowers and empty the mailbox for each other, or we chat when we go shopping, we meet on the way, slowing down a bit and chatting. There is contact among very old people who have been living here from the beginning, and younger ones whom I speak to off my own bat. I speak to people, ask them whether they live, here, and if so, then you know about them, then you can open the door or the door of the lift for them, and you can get into a conversation, and this way the new tenants themselves learn to be a bit friendlier and not so cold, so reserved.

45

SW *Do you feel there are new people coming and you have contact with these new people?*
Frau J Well, I try to establish contact with newcomers so that they won't feel so alien and one gets to know each other better in the house, because otherwise, if nobody says anything, one doesn't get to know each other and everybody avoids one another. It's simply better if you know each other and know we live in the same house and therefore we say at least hello and later perhaps a bit more.

SW *One thing that interests me greatly is that the house was a modern house, the ideal of modern. Inside with these wooden things, these cabinets, it's more old, there's a difference – old and not old. Is this something you did consciously?*
Frau J This is my taste, it just depends on what sort of taste you have. There are people who have a taste, everything quite modern, but I mix all of this, a bit modern, a bit old, and I just like it this way because it looks cosier than very modern furniture or such like, it's so angular and straight, and I don't like that so much.

SW *Did you have several stages towards this? Did you have to go slowly to make it?*
Frau J Slowly. I have done everything slowly. Since it simply costs a lot of money, you can't afford everything at once, and besides, it's more fun if you think things over – what can I do about the room, how can I do it, what colour matches – and then you buy the things bit by bit.

SW *All the flats are different in this block, so do you feel a sense of this difference? Do you feel that your flat is different from other ones around you, or do you think there's a similarity?*
Frau J Well, I like it that the flats are different. Although it's the same layout, it always gives me pleasure when I visit friends or neighbours, I see that one can do something quite different with the flat from what I have done myself, and I like that, and you can see from that that everyone has a different taste. One person needs lots of wardrobes to put all their stuff in, like myself. I never know where to put

all my stuff, and there are people who haven't got such a lot of stuff and they don't need all that many wardrobes, and so they put up fewer. So every flat is different, and I like that.

Andreas Jacob, 25 July 1992

SW *Can you describe what you think are the most important changes in the flat?*
AJ What has changed most for the better in the house are the entrances, they are no longer as dark as they used to be, they're brighter. When you come to the entrance now, everything is brighter, the colours are friendlier, there's always light so you don't have to fumble for the light switch; the light is switched on in each storey. Also the house has got cleaner, at the beginning it was dirtier and was often bedaubed, something that nowadays almost never happens, only very rarely, and there have been many changes inside the flats from the initial grey-on-grey, slowly some colour got there.

SW *Do you think in way that the house is more anonymous than it was before, devoid of any human qualities? Do you think there is less community here now?*
AJ Ah well, communication isn't all that great anymore because the people that move out, you still chatted to them, but those who move in now, you might meet them down at the entrance but that's about it. So there are only few people left that you can talk to. Especially the older ones, they're all dying on us.

SW *Do you think that the environment has changed? Looking at this sculpture, this metal modern art sculpture, what did you feel about that? Do you think it fits with this modern building, this modern art?*
AJ That thing hasn't even got any connection with the houses, the way it looks. You brand it as modern and that's good and that's expensive – that's all – and the houses are simply modern too, they say, and monotonous. They should rather put a showcase there with a model estate or something like that, something you can look at, it's more effective.

SW *What do you think of the drawings that children make around the house now?*
AJ It's horrible. It doesn't look good, and I'm of the opinion that those who paint that should, if you catch them, remove it. But unfortunately, when you catch them, their parents are so mindless they consult their solicitors and sue at any length, instead of being understanding and settling it through the insurance so that this corner will get a fresh coat of paint, which in the case of a personal liability insurance wouldn't even lead to a higher premium.

SW *So do you think that this* Wernerheim, *this life in the house, is like the life of the future?*
AJ Not inside the flat, the way it's laid out. But there are other flats that are more suitable for that because they are better laid out, and I'm of the opinion, if you lay it all out more clearly, brightly and appealingly, it will certainly be the future way of life, if only because you can squeeze an incredible number of people into a small space. If everything is thoroughly thought out and the infrastructure put together well, I would say that this is the solution of the future.

SW *What kind of things do you do on your computer, do you play games or do you have competitions or do you do problems?*
AJ There are all sorts of things that you can do with computers, for instance, my neighbour collects stamps, he's got a kind of inventory to find out which ones he's got, which ones he needs, what value the collection has and so on and so forth. Every now and again I provide parts for the people I know, cheaply. I write programs for problem solving for my neighbour, this thing with the stamps. Just now I'm writing for someone else a program for a workshop. I also write texts, whatever comes up, or do things for fun for other people, doing some graphics, anything.

Von Einer Generation zur Nächsten, *January 1992/ January 1993, two panel work, 127cm high by 76.5cm wide. Photographic prints, photographic dye, acrylic paints, Letraset text on paper and card*

Klaus and Frau Müller, June 1979

SW *I'm on the eleventh floor at 120 Fritz-Erler Allee, talking to Klaus and Frau Müller. What kind of house did you live in before you came here and what made you come to a place like Gropius Stadt? Was it a very different kind of place?*

Frau M We always used to have flats with outdoor or bad toilets. This is our fifth flat in ten years. Our son had a kidney illness and so we absolutely wanted to get out of these cold and bad flats. This is why we moved here.

SW *Do you always go to Neukölln for your shopping?*

Frau M No, but if you want special items such as buttons, buckles and ribbon, then you're badly off. These are odds and ends – you have to get them in the big stores. Here in the tower there is a hairdressers that I used to go to, but then I went to Neukölln because there they only charge half the price for the same service and they are very nice. The one below I don't really like.

Herr M And if you want to buy something, if you forgot something, you have to walk ten minutes to buy it. That's the only thing that bothers me, that you first have to run a stretch to get it. Take half a pound of sugar or the salt you forgot. It takes me from ten minutes up to a quarter of an hour to get there, and then back again.

SW *What about social amenities, you know, places to go socially, are there many places around here that you can go to?*

Frau M None at all around here.

Herr M Around here next to nothing. Downstairs there's an inn. Only when I really fancy a draught beer, I go down for drink, but this is only once in a blue moon. Otherwise social amenities are only for youths, they have got their own tea room, but for older people there is nothing in particular.

SW *Can you think of any particular things about tower block life?*

Frau M We live on our own, don't we?

Herr/Frau M We are an island.

Herr M Something has changed . . .

Frau M You don't have neighbours any more.

Herr M It's not like it used to be in Neukölln when someone calls in and says: 'Let's have coffee together'. We miss that a lot; there's no community at all here. Here we say 'Guten Tag' and exchange a few words on the path or staircase, but otherwise . . .

Klaus and Frau Müller, September 1979

SW *I'm sitting with Klaus Muller and his wife in their flat, Fritz-Erler Allee, Gropius Stadt. I'd like to carry on more about your feelings, about living up here in the sky. First of all I wondered how you both felt about being so far away from the ground?*

Frau M I like living so high up. You can see over the houses, have a better view and then somehow I don't feel so encaged as if I was living so far down.

Herr M It's the same with me. We both like a good view. We have lived too long in a dark flat, yes, where we had to face the Berlin wall. We had the wall right outside our window, we lived on the ground floor at the second courtyard and when I compare this to here, sure it's completely different now, being able to look over everything.

SW *I just wondered if when you're sitting on your own sometimes or when you're in the flat, if you ever felt somehow isolated by the position you are in, just physically?*

Frau M Well, I can't say there's a lot happening here, no surprises. For instance somebody might ring the bell and a friend would be calling. You don't experience this, everybody who calls has informed us beforehand.

SW *Do you ever feel that the fixed nature of the concrete environment inhibits you in any way in making contacts with other people?*

Frau M Yes, of course. If you compare this environment with the inner city where we used to live, you find shops and stores there and people in the streets. You don't find this here, nobody walks the streets at night, the only thing you see is cars moving around.

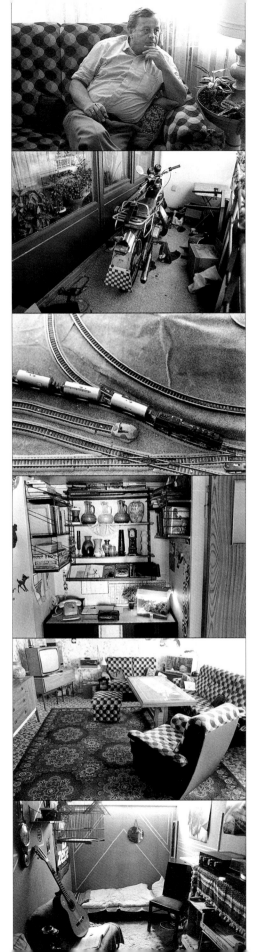

Herr M At 6pm the pavements are 'folded up' and then it's dead silent, the dance of the dead. If my wife wasn't here, yes, I think I could feel very lonely.

Frau M If I didn't feel like seeing anybody or have the strength to go out, yes, then it's very lonely.

SW You've got such a particular kind of physical environment which you live in. I just wondered how you felt about the structure of the tower which might affect you making contacts with people all around you?

Herr M You only make contacts in the lift. You meet them there, you exchange a few words with a few people but you wouldn't call it friendship, just a fleeting acquaintance.

SW Do you think the environment of the tower is a contributing factor towards the gangs of kids, graffiti and vandalism you experience?

Frau M Not so much in this form but I'm very scared that they might get involved in some gangs where they take drugs. I really fear this as I know that my kids have reached a dangerous age for that; they are still clean but I'm still very scared. The kids go to clubs here and every youngster meets there and amongst them also you find the drug addicts. If they find a drug dealer, they would take him away, I know that, but to find the dealer first seems very difficult. The boys' ages in the club range from fourteen to twenty-one years on average. Our boys joined the club when they were fifteen. The little one seems very involved, he's sixteen now and he tries very hard to find contact with other boys there. He's got some common sense for sure, he always talks about everything when he gets home but I'm still very frightened. It only needs an unhappy love affair or something to make them unhappy and then something might happen. Clubs belong to the school and the church. You find the worst club in the church, they've closed this one down already three times.

SW How do you think the room at the top of the tower could be used to create more of a community here?

Frau M The room at the top of the tower has been used a few times, but only for family celebrations, private parties. You can only use the room for these purposes or, for instance, when my son's schoolmates were having a party here, we hired the room, but otherwise you wouldn't meet anybody up there. There's nowhere in the block where you could have some social gathering. We would welcome it very much if there was a table tennis room or something like that, somewhere where people can meet. The ground floor hasn't been constructed very well; they could have built some communal rooms but nobody cares.

SW Do you think the room could be used more than it is?
Frau M If the room wasn't for hire I would put some table tennis boards or something similar in there. I would love to play table tennis and a lot of the young people here in the house would enjoy games. It's not only for the sake of playing games but also you could meet your neighbours that way.
Herr M You could, for example, organise some gathering for elderly people, but to do anything like that somebody has to take the initiative. Let me just tell you one incident concerning the lifts. After they'd been scribbled on, I'd made the suggestion to buy some Hornitex and repair the walls. I even offered to do it.

SW What do you think one could do to adapt the environment in some way here to mould your own needs to your idea of a community?
Herr M You could do something with the help of the housing administration but you always need somebody who takes the initiative. For example, you could let the room on the top to be at anybody's disposal just once every four weeks and then organise a coffee round inviting everybody to take part. I'm convinced that one third would come. The second time a second third would join and so forth. The suggestion could come from any tenant, but everything else must be taken over by the housing administration. It's impossible to finance this out of our own pockets.

Frau M Our landlords once suggested a children's party for all the kids in the area, it could all be possible but you need financial support otherwise it just remains an idea.

SW Do you feel that the flat has really changed your own behaviour between yourselves, has it influenced the way you go about doing things?
Frau M No, the only change I've noticed in me is that I've become more restless, which shows in going out a lot more, my husband also. When I'm alone and feel bored, I take the car or go by underground to Neukölln; I wouldn't stay here alone, I'd feel uneasy. This never happened in our old flat before. We had a lot of visitors but without all my friends here I sometimes feel lost and forgotten. I'm sure this has something to do with living in this area, nothing to do with our flat. We really like our flat.
Herr T I feel the same about being alone here. I've got to go out when my wife's working; I take a walk or go to Neokölln just to do something. It's better than sitting around here doing nothing and feeling alone.

SW Do you ever feel the lifts constitute a barrier between your inner world in the flat and your outer world around you? Is it a sort of buffer between the inner and outer worlds?
Frau M Our lift is the main topic for the people in the block. Firstly, because it is always late. Sometimes you wait for the lift longer than waiting for the U-Bahn, and secondly all the scribbling on the walls. You know who's done it. The landlord doesn't seem to bother about it, doesn't even talk to the kids' parents. Why can't the parents pay for the damage? They have to be made responsible, but nothing has been done about it so far. It's been like this for half a year.

SW Do you ever feel frustrated with the very fixed nature of the environment, that you can only change your own behaviour to meet the nature of the environment?
Frau M Yes, I sometimes dream of having a jolly party on our floor inviting everybody, preparing a beautiful banquet and I'm sure

A sequence viewed from above, L to R of In Isolation Leben, *May 1979/January 1980, four panel work*

everybody would get to know each other. We could invite the people from upstairs and downstairs, too so that nobody could complain about the noise.

Herr M We've never had difficulties meeting people, like our New Year's party when we rang the bell at our neighbours and asked them to have a glass of champagne with us. As far as we're concerned we really do our best, our neighbours seem to like us and the children, at Christmas the kids always get something.

Frau M In the block everybody would like some contact but I'm sure you can put it down to being shy and inhibited. They just don't dare to invite anybody.

Eine Postmoderne Lebensform

In Isolation Leben was made with Klaus Müller in Gropius Stadt between 1978 and 1979. He lived in the huge tower block that stands at 120 Fritz-Erler Allee. It was therefore with great anticipation that I revisited the tower in 1992 and meet Torsten Müller, the son of the original participant.

Revisiting a previous context for a work to conceive a new one is not something I have often done before, and therefore it is interesting that the outcome from my new involvement was to be so different. While the internal environment of the flat had been largely unaltered – or seemed that way to me – from my first visit, and was thus a constant connection with the past, the personal orientation of the son was firmly directed to the future. This conception of the future took as its baseline the normality of 'modernism' inherent in the physical fabric of the building and surrounding environment: the participant is from a generation brought up in Gropius Stadt that has experienced nothing else.

While the environment created by his parents lingers on, with its clear reference to the past, and a way of life symbolised by the tower block, the son has no such nostalgia. He has created a contrasting world of personal objects to form a network that has a contrasting message for the environment in which they are all contained.

While this work is located in the same context as my previous piece the message has become quite different, and while it reflects the passage of time it is also states a new generation's separation from the past, and provides a means of looking at the personal future of the individual.

Torsten Müller, 25 October 1992

SW I'm very interested, because your generation may be the first to live all their life in a building like this. Did you feel it was a normal way of life? It's something planned. I wonder if you've responded to that open plan, whether you felt liberated, or maybe constrained by it or maybe whether you took no notice of it?

TM I'd say perhaps it's quieter here than it is in the inner city. You get some peace here. Trouble is, if you want to see life – and as a young person you do want to see a bit of life – then you've got to get away, by taking the underground and going into town, and then maybe you can see some life. Go to a film, a disco, a theatre, or whatever. But this is just a dormitory town. It's quite different. There's not much going on here.

SW Are there no clubs happening locally?

TM Yes, well, there are – or I should say there were – youth clubs. Still are, but the way I see it, there's not much to be said for being in those youth clubs. There's no one to supervise in a big way, people get some stupid ideas. There are a lot of young people who scrawl on the walls, and take it into their heads to do idiotic things. Because here, a youth club isn't everything. You've got to have space to move, and that just doesn't happen here.

SW Do you think this is maybe how you got into the computer? You're in this kind of capsule, and somehow it seems the computer opens to a bigger world, a mental room?

TM It makes a change. You can be in a capsule, cut off from the world. It works. When the phone rings, of course I get up. You can

do just the same thing with a book; that's a medium too. You need something to relax with, cut yourself off with. You need some peace. And this happens to be one medium I need for that purpose.

SW *Do you find the computer puts you forward, that it extends you outwards into a kind of network, that maybe the computer makes a kind of social relationship for you?*
TM Network, that's right, or rather, through the computer I've made a lot of friends. It's not like that, because you compare notes, and so on. And here there happen to be a lot of people who are into computers, and you soon get to know each other. That way you also make new friends. That's how I see the network.

SW *So the computer itself is very cerebral, a kind of enclosed experience, but it actually extends your social network at the same time?*
TM Yes, I'd say the computer is turning more and more into something absolutely normal. People are growing up with computers. I had my hands on a computer for the first time when I was thirteen, and it's getting more normal all the time. So I'd say, you don't just shut yourself away with a computer, you build up contacts. It becomes normal, as normal as a book, a telephone or whatever. You grow up with it.

SW *Do you think that the computer is a symbol of modern life, because here we are in a tower which could be a symbol of that? I'm also interested in this being a tower, so maybe there's a connection.*
TM That's all design. And I'd say, it's all tending towards a Manhattan skyline style, but I think it's probably going to go a lot further. For instance, the built-in cupboards start to look like a tower block. It's all going in the same direction. I do think people are slowly going to find their way back to something that's got more warmth. It's already happening, the Renaissance look and so on.

SW *Another thing I noticed, you have weights here. Do you feel that somehow it's very*

OVERLEAF: Eine Postmoderne Lebensform, *July 1992/ February 1993, two panel work, 76.5cm wide by 126cm high. Photographic prints, photographic dye, acrylic paint and Letraset text on card*

ES IST SOWEIT NORMAL, ICH KENNE
DAS ANDERE LEBEN HALT NUR VON ERZÄHLUNGEN

MAN WÄCHST AUF, INTERESSEN ÄNDERN SICH,
ABER ALLE SIND GENAUSO GEBLIEBEN, WIE SIE WAREN

important to do physical things in here, to exercise yourself in this space? Do you sometimes feel distanced from outside?
TM No, I wouldn't say that. Perhaps I'd make a connection here, between weightlifting and this building, or this life. It's just normal for me to have something to do. And this is what suggests itself because I've tried out various kinds of sport: swimming, for instance and karate. I don't see it in relation to life here.

SW Is the landscape very important to you? The view, the trees, things like this?
TM Yes, it's very important to me. Again, it's the contrast, between white and black, instead of grey you need this green. That's important.

SW Do you use the green areas a lot? Do you find yourself in the woods?
TM I use it, all right. I often go down there,

56

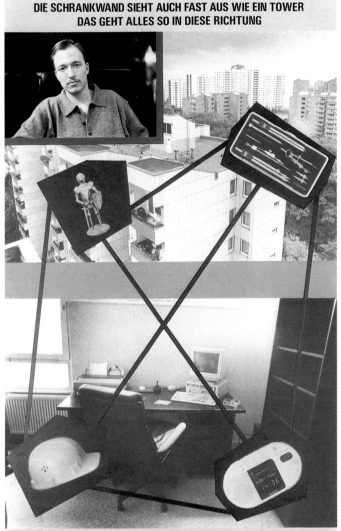

DIE SCHRANKWAND SIEHT AUCH FAST AUS WIE EIN TOWER
DAS GEHT ALLES SO IN DIESE RICHTUNG

ICH WILL ES NICHT ALS IRGENDWELCHE MATTSCHEIBE SEHEN. ICH KANN
JA DAS FENSTER AUFMACHEN, DANN KANN ICH ALLES SPÜREN

look around a bit. For instance, behind here there's a bit of woodland being replanted. It's good to see the trees growing. And everyone needs a bit of movement. I like going down there.

SW *It's interesting that you talked about black and white. Is that something you want to extend, or just something you did because*

it was in a magazine? Did you think about making things very contrasting?
TM No, I didn't see the black and white in a magazine. I just think it looks really neat. The kind of contrast I really like. For instance, I'm making my flat at home black and white again, this living room, but in the bedroom I'd like something different, I'd like pine. A restful sort of space.

Pat Purdy and the Glue-Sniffers' Camp

The Avondale Estate at Hayes in West London was built in the mid-1960s and was a product of the Hillingdon Council planning department's concept at the time for 'model' low-cost, high-density housing. It was a concept that has since gone disastrously wrong, and now a great many flats are simply unin-habitable – the sole preoccupation of remaining tenants is to get out as fast as possible.

On arriving in London at the end of 1980 from West Berlin, I started to look around West London and I returned to the Avondale Estate, where I met the leader of the unofficial tenants' association, Mrs Briggs. She introduced me to ten other tenants, mostly elderly, who she felt were trying to fight back against their environment, but I was becoming more and more interested in the reactions of younger people who had been brought up on the estate, as this would be the only reality that they would know.

While I was talking with a Mrs Purdy she suggested her daughter Pat might be interested in co-operating with me. What transpired from my conversations and later taped discussions with Pat Purdy, was the great importance of the wasteland, known as the 'Lurky Place', that lay directly adjacent to the estate. From walking around the wasteland with Pat and discussing what she did there, I came to realise the central role that building camps had for the teenage youth population living on the estate. The structure of the piece emerged after a number of meetings with Pat Purdy, when I photographed her environment on the estate and made a number of taped discussions. The work is equally divided between the deterministic pressures emitting from the estate, and the wasteland; seen as the context for resisting those pressures by creating a counter-consciousness. Having developed the basic structure, I revisited one camp that Pat had been particularly associated with, photographed it, and then removed at her suggestion all the discarded objects I could find. I decided to embody the collection of objects found in the camp directly in the work, and asked Pat to write her own quotations straight on to the photographic panels.

The work is developed around four functions of the wasteland as seen by Pat: relieving tension, establishing self-identity, expressing own values and formation of a community. Each state is made up of a tryptich with the left panel centring on a particular pressure emitting from the new reality, the centre panel located on the boundary between the two realities and the right panel expresses the freedom found in the wasteland.

Pat Purdy, 30 January 1981

SW *How would you first of all describe this estate in your own words?*
PP Sometimes it either goes from absolutely dead quiet as it is now, to raving rows, lunatics, smashes, guns – the lot, but apart from that there's nothing else, that's about the excitement for the year.

SW *How would you describe the actual physical layout, you know, what are the buildings like?*
PP The buildings, they're like shoe boxes with windows, that's all. I'd just say everybody that I've brought back here . . . the amount of people who've turned round and said, 'Oh, it's like walking into a prison block,' which I suppose it is, not having been in one before, but so many people have said that.

SW *So would you say that things have changed round here in that amount of time?*
PP They've changed in the sense that I don't know anybody here anymore; when I was younger there were loads of people that I knew, I was very rarely at home, I could, in the morning, get up, go and make the breakfast in the kitchen, look out the window and just start chatting to somebody from the window. Now I look out the window and I don't know any-body, so it's changed in a community sense. I don't know anybody at all, when I'm at home I stay in and that's it, the only people who come knocking on the door are my friends from off of the estate but no friends on the estate.

SW *What sort of things did you do when you were quite little, I mean you had quite a lot of friends here then?*
PP Yes, loads of them we used to, in the summer we'd get up about eight, be out the house by eight thirty till six o'clock at night, we'd go to the fields at the back – they were all open then – we'd go over there and build camps and sit round smoking, take a tin of baked beans and and either cook the tin of baked beans on a little camp fire or just eat them cold.

SW *Would you say that wasteland had some sort of importance for the kids on the estate?*
PP Yes, yes it was somewhere where we could all go, scream, shout, do anything we wanted and nobody knowed, the only person who ever minded was the bloke who had the scrapyard where we used to go and nick old car seats.

SW *The old car dismantlers?*
PP Yes, we used to go and nick car seats to make the camps; pieces of metal, wood and things, but other than that there was nobody about who could moan at us and it was somewhere we could go to be on our own and enjoy ourselves.

SW *But when did you first become aware of it, when did you first start going in there?*
PP When I first heard of it it was always known as 'the track' and the big lads, the greasers, used to go there with their bikes, so I never went near it; I thought it was just for the big boys. I think there was one summer holiday I went over with a friend, her brother used to go over there, he was one of the greasers and he used to go over there so she was allowed to go with him. So I went along one day, we just sat over there and then we started going over there regularly; we sat there watching the blokes riding their bikes and then we started going over there regu-larly, and then we started to go and build camps with car seats and that and build camps and it all grew on from there.

SW *So it's predominantly for kids, that kind of thing?*
PP Yes, which is why we liked it so much, as I say, there was nobody to complain about us screaming, shouting, running around.

SW *And what would you say were the main things that went on there, I mean the kind of activities, apart from track bikes?*
PP Just us building the camps and strolling around and sitting round talking and smoking and, just mainly set on building the camp and adding bits to it and painting it up and then when we'd done one bit of work, we'd sit down

and have something to eat and sit there the rest of the day, chatting and talking, it was a meeting place and somewhere we could relax.

SW *I'm interested in the contrast between this place and that place because it's only a couple of hundred yards away.*
PP Yes, it's not that far away, I can't really see it from this window, I suppose that's why I like it over there so much 'cos I can't see it from this window; the only views I've got from all the windows in the house is of another block that's exactly the same as the one I'm living in, and you see someone else looking out the window and it's like looking in a mirror.

SW *So, the kids though that go over, are they just from this estate or . . . where do they come from?*
PP Used to be mainly from this estate and a couple of roads that run next to ours, the railway estate, but it was mainly from this estate: there were loads of us running around.

SW *Did you have territories which you used to defend?*
PP No, no, we didn't, we all pretty much mucked in together. I'd say we had about two camps going, I think there was some strange kids, I remember going to the camp one day and it was all broken and battered and somebody had been in there and smashed it up and we never found out who it was, but we happened to find these other camps built that we didn't know about so we moved in there ourselves and moved our gear in and slung the other stuff out, and we used it and I can't remember who it belonged to but we felt it was probably them that broke up our camp, so we went and moved into theirs.

SW *Can you describe for us the difference in how you see the place between, ten years ago and now?*
PP The grass was longer ten years ago, it was a meeting place then, seemed to have more life and a life of its own then, whereas now it's just a piece of scrap land; just a bit of land that's doing nothing. Everything's

deteriorating. There's trees been pulled down over there, there's a whole clump of trees that've been pulled down over there that were beautiful. It was lovely when I first started going over there, there were a lot more bushes and trees, whereas now it just seems to be gradually flattened out, I think its going to be flattened out and end up like this place in the end.

SW *Do you think life on the estate's better with it there for the kids or whoever uses it?*
PP Yes, if they opened it up – they fenced it all off – when I used to go there it wasn't fenced off at all.

SW *Oh, there was no fence?*
PP No, there was no fence; all that's pretty recent, the council built a pathway through it, fenced it off, we used to walk over, but now the kids have to cut holes in fences. If they opened it up again and let the kids over there, they'd feel a bit more free and probably a lot more of them would go over there and build camps and live more over there than they do on the estate, but with it being fenced off, a lot of the parents tell them not to go over there.

SW *What about older people, what do you think they could do over there or do you think they could benefit?*
PP Take the dogs for walks instead of taking them round the estate and people complaining about them being on the estate just go out for walks, on there 'cos it's lovely really, especially when, when you get down by the canal but they've got a nice little brook thing out there and what with the canal and going fishing and that they should open it up and let the kids get a bit of benefit from it, because, at least it's got a bit of natural form to it which the estate hasn't, it's a basic square. The trees are put in where they should be, the paths all run square, there's no curves in the paths on the estate either, the only curve's in the road.

Pat Purdy and Ann Tuffin, 28 March 1981

SW On the first tape you were talking about these places being like shoe boxes, well that interested me, and I was just wondering if you could elaborate: how do you think they are like shoe boxes, what makes you say that?

PP It's the shape, the sizes of them and the way everything's . . . they look as though the architect has just thought of shoe boxes and laid them on the site and just tried to organise us into these shoe boxes; even the rooms are just completely square. I get the feeling on this estate that there's no nice curves or anything round, everything's just square and cold, even the rooms inside the house are square there's no nooks and crannies and little places or anything.

AT One way out, like a shoe box; your front door, that's the only way out.

SW Are you conscious of the fact that the architect is trying to tell you how to live?

PP Yes, he's tried to organise the life here but he's not been able to organise it around anything central. We've got a big green that the kids are supposed to play on, but they've taken the swings away from there; they've only got a seesaw left and you can't have any community feeling when there's nowhere for people to meet and to communicate, which there isn't on this estate. You just drift along the corridor and doors are closed: the architect has tried to organise our life here but he's not worked it out properly.

SW Do you feel like you're being constrained then?

AT Yes, it is like being in prison, in a way isn't it, and when we were younger we weren't allowed to go off the estate.

PP The bits of green down there in between the blocks, you're not allowed to play football, the kids aren't allowed to play football on those greens they've got one green and one green only to play football on. Not allowed to play on the little bits of green in between, which is controlling us and and trying to keep us down, trying to keep the kids down and I'd say if the kids are outside playing and the way

the noise travels around these places you can hear it, the further up you go the louder you can hear it, there's just no break from it at all.
AT The only place we could go really was over the track 'cos you could shout, scream, do what you wanted to do without anyone shouting out the window, 'Shut up!' You know, even out in the park we used to be out there and all kids, you know, make a bit of a racket but half eight at night and they shouted out the windows, this is summer when it's light, it's awful, you're really restricted.

SW *When you went over the track, were you aware at all of being surrounded by factories?*
PP No, never used to think of it, never used to think of that, we just used to go over there.
AT No, no, it was a way out, to sort of relieve our feelings in a way, wasn't it, relieve the tension?
PP It was, we just went over there to get away from everything and we forgot about everything, forgot about this place.
AT Yes, it was like another little world really, wasn't it?
PP Never thought about this place over there.

SW *No, but I mean when you were sitting in the middle, were you aware it was a special place?*
PP No, because there was so much going in within it, you didn't think of what was going on outside and I suppose there was a lot more foliage around there so it was like being in deep woods or something.
AT Yes, you couldn't really see the flats from there.

SW *Can you describe a camp that you built then, I mean, what did they look like?*
PP It would consist of . . .
AT . . . them sheets of corrugated iron . . .
PP . . . sheets of corrugated iron that we'd get from the . . .
AT . . . scrapyard . . .
PP . . . scrapyard, a couple of car seats, we used to try and get the best we could, although we used to run over there and just grab whatever's nearest we used to sort of be a bit fussy and try not to get something too

ripped up or in too much of a state, there'd be a couple of double car seats in there, all centred round a little fireplace thing and just the corrugated iron. It's pretty basic but we had somewhere to sit down and we'd try to sort of cover it over as best we could if the weather was a bit dodgy, but mainly it was open. I only remember one that was actually covered over with the corrugated iron.

SW *What, sort of like a roof?*
PP Yes, we used to mainly put the corrugated iron round the sides to block off the wind and block off people seeing us and that.

SW *What kind of objects did you used to take over there, can you remember?*
PP We didn't take any personal belongings 'cos we couldn't, it was so open, anyone could walk in and take it. We'd just take cigarettes, a tin of baked beans and bread and butter, that's about all we'd take over, we didn't take any personal things over and make them into little homes or anything, they were just somewhere to go and sit down and have your bread and beans.

SW *But I suppose you would take matches?*
PP Yes, knives, penknives used to go over there 'cos we used to play chicken with the penknives, I can't remember radios over there.

SW *So there must have been some sort of organisation in the gang, some kind of formal structure.*
PP Well, there was Pat and Brian Luck, brother and sister, and Brian Luck – all the blokes used to meet round his house and they were very quiet but because they were quiet they sort of held an air of authority and we all sort of were a bit worried about if they lost their temper what they'd do, so they held a bit of authority and Pat Luck held a bit of authority with the girls, and also 'cos they came from right in London – Paddington or somewhere – we considered them to be really hard, but they were mainly little ringleaders.

SW *Well, what were the sort of things you used to talk about then I mean, when you were*

just sitting around the camps?
PP That's awkward.
AT Quite an awkward question, isn't it?
PP Who you fancied . . .
AT That's right, yes.

SW *Well, yes, just those kinds of things.*
AT Who was going out with so-and-so.
PP Where you'd hidden your packet of fags at home, and what your Dad said about what the time you got in last night, being ten minutes late.

SW *How do you think that place released tensions on the estate?*
PP It got us off the estate. If we had any little fights or quarrels we could have them over there, you'd get nobody looking out the window saying, 'Stop fighting, stop shouting, stop screaming', we didn't feel that our parents could walk round the corner anytime, 'cos very rarely did our parents come over there looking for us, so we didn't feel that they would walk round the corner any minute and find us doing something that . . .
AT . . . shouldn't do, yes.
PP So, so that relaxed us a bit, just getting off of the estate.

SW *Do you ever think it made you feel more like fighting back against this place, if you didn't have that place?*
PP Well, in the bad weather during the winter months we'd have to hang about here; we didn't go over to the fields and we'd hang about on the stairs, and the corridors and sit there and freeze to death on the stairs. Then you'd just start writing on the stairs, something to do, we'd just sit around on the stairs, slip in the corridors and you'd get somebody coming out saying, 'Get out the corridor and take your dog ends with you'.
AT So you'd go along to the next block and then someone'd come out . . .
PP We'd just wander from block to block around the corridors and sit on the stairs, or sit in the sheds.
AT Yes, down the sheds.
PP Down in the sheds in those hallway pieces there.

SW *A lot of people talk about kids, vandalism, breaking up the estate – that's the typical thing older people come up with. Why do you think you used to draw on the walls?*
PP When I was hanging about on the estate, you just sit there and start talking and you got a lot of energy in you that you can't expel anywhere, you sit and you start fidgeting . . .
AT Before you know what you're doing you've got a pen . . .
PP . . . And then you you pick something up or start on something, you start scratching into something; it's just nerves and you build up, you've got so much energy to expel and there's nowhere to do it, nowhere to do it. It would have made a big difference in the summer, it would have done definitely, because we would just have hung around on the estate and probably ripped it apart.

SW *But what about the boundary between there and here, I mean, what's the ideal relationship, what would you like?*
PP What, now?

SW *Yes.*
PP I'd like them to take the fence down get a bit more foliage up in the fields because a lot of it's been cut down and ruined, it, it's getting a bit desolate there now, but just take the fence down and let the kids go over there and do what they like.
AT Do what they want.

SW *So you wouldn't like the separation?*
PP No, no, I don't.
AT No, just give them the land and say, well there's that bit of land, do what you like, just do what you want.
PP Just leave it and let them go.

A sequence of four triptychs viewed from above, L to R of Pat Purdy and the Glue-Sniffers' Camp, *January/September 1981, twelve panel work, eight panels 102cm wide by 76.5cm high, four panels 66cm high by 51cm wide. Photographic prints, photographic dye, gouache, Letraset text, ink, felt-tip pen and objects found by Pat in the Lurky Place, mounted on paper and card*

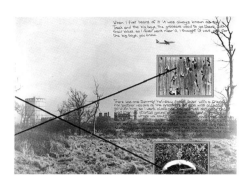
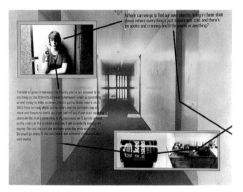

Taboo Housing Estate

One phenomenon of late 1970s London was the surfacing into the public realm of the dominant 'normal' culture of a counter-consciousness. Firmly held beneath the surface, it had broken out in the form of post-punk and its associated derivatives. For a moment there seemed to be a parallel world where you could hide from the determinism of society and completely immerse oneself. Having completed my work with Pat Purdy, I was exploring ways of developing the experience of the wasteland when I met an old friend on his way to visit the Cha Cha Club, situated in an obscure vault along the dark alleys beneath Charing Cross Station. The idea of a club – created by friends for friends, so that they could freely express a sensibility and attitudes that were tangential, even alien from the normality of the dominant culture – seemed immensely important, and consequently I met the organisers, Michael and Scarlett, to discuss creating a new work there.

Are You Good Enough For The Cha Cha Cha? (1982) was originally presented at the Lisson Gallery as part of the exhibition *Inside The Night*. Made with the active involvement of visitors to the club over a six-month period, the piece embodies the residue of objects I found on the floor after a night there. While working with Scarlett she mentioned her life on an estate in North Tottenham where she had managed to get a council flat. Living under the cover of darkness, coupled with her overt expression of a counter-consciousness, meant that she demonstrated quite a different approach to the estate environment, so I suggested that the context of her flat could be a vital catalyst for the generation of another work.

The resulting *Taboo Housing Estate* was quickly made by myself and Scarlett on the floor of her living room, using objects we found there, together with text that she wrote directly on to the piece. The work has an underlying commentary about 'modern art', and the background is formed from two shapes reminiscent of Russian Constructivism. The voodoo head fixed next to the front door was made by Scarlett, and attracted or repelled, depending on which side of the normative fence the onlooker fell.

Scarlett, 16 December 1982

SW *First of all we're going to talk about your life in this flat at night; how's it feel to be the bogeywoman on this estate?*
S Well, I'm not actually the bogeywoman anymore. I was the bogeywoman when I first moved in 'cos everybody hated me, but you know, I'm an accepted member of the community these days, 'cos I never see anybody, except in the pub, and they go out once a week, Fridays and Saturdays to booze, always the same people, always the same days, but apart from that I never see anyone.

SW *So, yes, you're living here on your own – tell us a bit about it?*
S When I first moved in I hated it 'cos I hated living here and I hated living on my own 'cos I'd never lived on my own before, but fortunately I have a dog which takes my mind off a lot of things and compensates for a person. Also it's 'cos I live very differently to other people: I'm up most of the night and sleep most of the day so it doesn't really, like other people around me, affect me very much at all because they're not up when I'm up.

SW *What do you think of the estate at night?*
S Oh the estate's great at night because, oh it's lovely 'cos if you're coming in or going out there's just no one around. It's not sort of, you know, when you're walking down the street and there's no one there and you feel scared. You just don't feel frightened 'cos there's just no, the crime rate is nil around here practically; there's been about two muggings in five years, there's no one around anyway and then you get in or you get up or something and by about ten o'clock you look out of your window and there's one light on. You just look out and you're the only one there; you go out and walk up and down and there's just no lights on.

SW *Just coming back to this flat, what sort of environment have you tried to create here? How's it different from the flat next door?*
S Well, it's very different, you're brought up and your tastes are supposed to be like this, and your mother wants you to have the same

tastes as she does and therefore with most people, generally their living room resembles their mother's, perhaps it might be a little bit trendier or younger, but it does resemble their mother's and this just doesn't at all. I just like red, it reminds me of a womb this room, that's why I like it.

SW What, you're trying to make it like that?
S No, I just like red, I just always wanted a red room, always, and everyone said to me, you know, if you have a red room it's sup-posed to be very dangerous and you won't be able to sit in there very long and it gives you headaches. Well, this is actually my favourite room of the whole flat, just 'cos it's very comfortable, it does remind me of a brain or a womb or, you know, something very warm and pumping inside your body that's actually living and it's just, you know, it's comfy.

SW What, you feel comfortable?
S Yes definitely.

SW But do you think it expresses something about you?
S In a way, yes, 'cos it's something that I always wanted to do, which is why I did it in a way, the number of people that say, you know, 'That room is disgusting', or, 'How could you live there?', but the thing is, I can actually live here very comfortably, and so in that way I think yes, it does, because it's something that I like. It's not something that I've said: 'Alright, because everyone is saying you don't like it, I've got to say that I like it', I mean I do actually like it.

SW But what about the objects, where do you get the objects from?
S I find them – what did I buy? Nothing, oh, yes I did, I bought that red plant pot and that's the only thing I bought in this whole room. I find things on skips, I found nearly everything in this whole flat on the skip, this sofa I found in Earls Court when I was up there, I found that, the table, the record player somebody gave me, I found the chair, I found the ashtray, I found that chair, I found my red cups and, just everything.

SW So you just sort of go sniffing around?
S Well, there's brilliant skips you see, that's one good thing about living around here; because it's new and trendy they're trying to keep it very clean and nice and they don't like people dumping large pieces of furniture outside on the rubbish bins outside, so they provide skips at the end of every street and people just throw out really brilliant things, and they always tend to throw them out during the day so that everyone can see, you know, that they're throwing out something that really isn't necessary to throw out because they've got a new one, or they've got to be one better than everybody else, so I just run along and pick it all up behind them and paint it.

SW Tell us about the night then?
S The night's more exciting than the day. There's no one around, basically, and it's like what I said about people and not being particularly interested in what people around me in this sort of environment are doing. It's just, it's sort of exciting, it's dark and it's very exciting, very exciting indeed, it's when I start to come alive after about sort of eight o'clock at night, start coming alive, even if I'm just staying in. Some nights you'll go out but some night's obviously you don't and it's just much more fun to sit up all night, it does waste the electricity bills which is one bad thing about it, you spend more on your lights and your record player than you do during the day 'cos you keep it going for longer.

SW Do you feel more creative at night?
S Yes, I get inspired to do things, like even if I haven't got any money, if I've got a tin of red paint and something that needs painting or something, that I think well, I'll just do that and you know, splash about. Even if I've got no money, I can always find something to do at night, it's like I say, you can always just, get something, even something I've been mean-ing to do for ages and just sort of do them, like this entire room. When I moved in I painted the room, the room was red and the sofa was red and the chair was red, and that's about it, and I really did want everything to be red. 'Cos I was working when I was doing the club

and I was really busy and then one night I just had a fit, I had absolutely no money and I didn't go out for about the next two days so I just went out and got out the tin of paint and just had a fit on the room.

SW *You don't feel sort of free at night?*
S Yes, and also 'cos you can walk about the streets, I mean, it's much easier for me to take the dog out at night for example, I mean it's not – it's pretty dumb to say that it's safer 'cos it probably isn't because people do get mugged at night, but I don't know, it is much safer. There's a garage up the road that sells cigarettes and milk and stuff, so if you need to pop up there and buy things you can: it's open twenty-four hours which is okay, but even walking up there, I mean you can go up at eleven o'clock and there'll be no one around 'cos they go to bed so early.

SW *Because I wondered, this room, it's like a kind of capsule, isn't it?*
S Definitely, it's quite nice like that 'cos you can come in and you feel really sort of safe, it's all warm and safe and no one can touch me when I'm in here, it's like a sort of shell. I feel that if anything happened, anything at all, like the world could blow up and I'd still be sitting here in my little room, you know, with my dog and my cats.

SW *Do you feel sometimes aggressive about your surroundings?*
S Not so much anymore, I did, when I first moved in, I did feel terribly aggressive 'cos I had a lot of hassle from the neighbours and I had hassle from the kids, which especially annoyed me beyond belief, 'cos you can't really go up to child and beat its head in, not if it's six or seven years old. They were just extremely rude, but the thing is, people have sort of come to accept me quite a lot now, they'll talk to me in the pub and they'll talk to me in the shop and it's all, 'Hello, how are you?' and 'cos everyone round here is either sort of middle aged and old or they're young with kids, with all the old ones it's 'Hello, dear, how are you?' you know, and they're okay, it's just I can't really be bothered to stand round

talking to them, I don't mind saying hello, I just can't really be bothered to hang about.

SW *What do you think motivates you to do that, to actually stay up at night and 'live out' the night?*
S I don't know, but the night is definitely more exciting; you can go and visit people and you can get on the night bus and it'll be twelve thirty or something, 'cos a lot of my friends live similarly, where they'll be up till about three or four in the morning which is okay 'cos that means you pop out and see them latish, and just before they go to bed you can still get home on the bus, but I mean it's just more exciting, you walk up the street and it's just much, much more exciting. There's no one there, not a soul, nobody, and there's no one to scream at you or your funny hairdos and laugh at you. They just don't hassle you, there's no one to beat you up and if people do get heavy I've always got the dog. You can walk around with your dog on the lead through a bunch of skinheads and the chances are they wouldn't really say anything.

SW *Do you think things look better at night?*
S Yes, I mean they, they look literally better because people are darker, and people tend to look very plain and very ugly during the day and a lot of it has to do with the light, you see, especially sunlight – if you catch people walking in the sun they're sort of squinting their eyes everywhere; they just don't look very nice. At night they look much more relaxed and they look much better.

SW *You can live off it, I mean, how do you organise your . . .?*
S No, not really, I organise my money situation very well actually; I get the dole, take it, cash it, pay the rent, put some money aside which goes into a Post Office account for the bills, buy a telephone stamp so I've always got something to pay for the telephone – which leaves me practically nothing, then I go out buy two weeks' dog food, two weeks' cat food, which is about five pounds a week for the three of them, which isn't really that much; I know if I didn't have them I'd certainly be

much richer, but I have got them, that's all there is to it, it's just one of the responsibilities you have if you take them on. It costs me about a fiver to feed all three of them for a week, so I buy two weeks of that, haul it home and then go out the next day and just buy like two weeks' worth of veg and bread and things like that, just basic needs, and things like washing up liquid.

SW *But you did do some extraordinary things, like you made that voodoo head.*
S Yes, I just do things like that, I just have a whim, a whim to do things, like I decorated this, it was just a plain white blind and I didn't really want to paint it, but I suddenly had this whim to whip out the paint and do a few splashes, you know, and just little things like that. If I'm interested in something at the time I'll do it there and then; I can't bear to put anything off anyway, unless I don't really want to do it. If there's something that I want to do I'd rather travel six miles to go and buy some equipment that I might need to do it and do it that day, rather than wait till the next day. I just can't bear waiting for things, I'm a very impulsive person, I have to do things on impulse, and I think that's how you create things, whether it's from writing somebody a letter, a sort of exciting, creative letter or you know, creating something like the doll, if you don't do things on impulse you don't get anything done, and obviously with bigger things you have to sit down and think, right, how am I going to do it? But you get this this impulse to do something and you think, right, I'm going to do that. I think everybody does, but people don't realise it, it's just 'cos I do everything very boldly, you see, and that's why other people notice it more.

SW *Why do you think you do it very boldly?*
S 'Cos I'm a bold person, that's all. I'm just a very bold person, I like to be bold about things, I don't like to do things by halves because I like to be bold, I just boldly step in, risk my life.

How would you live on the Taboo Housing Estate?

Taboo Housing Estate, October 1982, one panel work, 145cm by 92cm wide. Photographic prints, pencil, ink, Letraset text, felt-tip pen and objects found by Scarlett, mounted on paper and card

What Is He Trying To Get At?
Where Does He Want To Go?

I met Leigh Bowery through the Cha Cha Club where he was a regular visitor in the early 1980s. At the time he was developing his 'Futurist' image and had already begun to evolve his approach as an artist in articulating the language of inter-personal presentation centring on himself as the artwork. He took these ideas much further later in the 1980s, but nevertheless, even in 1982 they resulted in the manifestation of very extreme personal imagery that had a far-reaching influence on the 'night world' of counter-consciousness in London.

Leigh had recently moved into a flat in Farrell House, a tower block off the Commercial Road in East London, when I first discussed the idea of working with him. Even though the environment I found there was relatively bare, I was struck by his creation of a capsule that was a strong statement to the self-organisation of a very creative person. There is no doubt in my mind that Leigh felt alienated from the world of normality, as expressed during the day, and preferred venturing forth from his lofty capsule at night. Consequently the work was structured between day (left panel) and night (right panel), centring on the different languages associated with each, although it is strongly indicated that the day is to prepare for life at night.

I taped several discussions with Leigh, from which he selected short texts which were then written out directly on to the artwork. In a similar manner, photographs, domestic objects and personal possessions were also embodied in the work, with final choices made by Leigh himself. I asked him to contribute an innovation of his own into the artwork that would symbolise his situation in the tower block, and he responded with a fluorescent tower constructed from breeze blocks, painted in his two favourite colours, and positioned between the two panels.

Leigh Bowery, 5 March 1984

SW I'm sitting in Leigh's flat in Farrell House, a tower block in East London. First of all, can you tell us a little bit about the flat itself, and how you came to live here?

LB Well, I'd been staying with Trojan, who also lives here, at this flat at St Paul's which was quite good, but just a one-bedroom flat, so we got on to a number of schemes and tried to get into this bigger place. Well, there was another boy at that time so we wanted a three-bedroomed flat and we sort of ended up pretending our front door was being burnt down, someone tipped petrol through our letter box, that the neighbours were hassling us and things like that, so eventually they got us this place. We only had to wait for about three months, which was quite good considering, and that's why we're here, and we've been here . . . the day we moved was . . . I think it was the end of January we moved here, so it's probably about four weeks now, yes, about four weeks since we moved in.

SW How do you feel about living in this environment, because it's so high up here, when you look out of that window you just see all those rows and rows of houses?

LB I know, sometimes I go out, like there's some weeks when I'll just go out till two o'clock nearly every night, I mean weeks of that. Sometimes I won't get up till four in the afternoon so it's dark always and that's quite good, I like that; and if I'm in here a lot and don't go out I really become aware of being outside the flat when I'm out. I feel as though I'm up in a tower here, 'cos I'm going about my business and we don't get touched by the outside too much once we're in here. But at the same time we look out of the windows and things like that and like the look of things and we get ideas from that, but when we're down in the street and we're looking up it's completely different, it's like we're really outside once we're outside.

SW But you've got a particular identity for yourself, every time I've seen you, you've been wearing these very expressive clothes,

what sort of sensibility do you think you're trying to express in yourself?

LB I don't know, maybe it's 'cos I'm working in fashion as well – it's partly that – it's quite over the top. I go out now and I don't really care, it sounds a bit primitive to say I want to shock people, but I do really.

SW Is there a definite image that you're trying to project?

LB Well, I get ideas from all over the place, like at the moment I'm mad on different things about Indian cultures. I'm also over the top about different aspects of 1970s clothes, like platforms, and then I really like things from outer space as well, and if I do this show in New York for Suzanne the collection will be called 'A Paki in Outer Space'. It's all mixed up but I wouldn't like to think that I'm doing something that someone's done exactly the same before. I think I've always tried to do something else.

SW Do you think people want to escape more now?

LB Well, there's enough reason to escape, and I do like futurist things, but at the same time, everyone seems to think about the future that it's going to be completely functional, you know, everything that's extra or just sort of elaborations, are going to be done away with, and I don't think that's true. All the things I like now, you can easily wear them and they're comfortable at the same time. There's a lot of unnecessary things on them, which is just detail and bits of creative things I just dab on which are . . . I think make it special, which is what it's all about.

SW Do you find that you tend to stay in here in the day time and you then go out at night?

LB It does happen quite a lot. I don't like going to Sainsbury's very much and I shaved my eyebrows off – I'd get up in the morning, and not bother drawing them on or anything, and all of a sudden I'd be really, really aware that people are staring at me, looking at my face and I'll get the milk as quick as I can and rush back. Before I go out now I take precautions; anything I've got which is really plain and drab, draw some fairly realistic eyebrows on and I may venture out, but sometimes if I'm a bit hung over the eyebrows come out looking like big caterpillars that would probably have been better if I'd left them off.

SW *Do you get a lot of hassle from people living around you?*
LB Yes, you do, I get on quite well with Indian people, they seem . . . I don't know if they understand me or they just aren't curious, but they're not offensive like the local school kids and the local lads. If there's a couple of them they'll sort of jeer at us a bit, but I suppose you get that, in the middle of the West End going out to a club, then I think we've got more reason to 'cos we're really dressed up.

SW *How do you manage to live, do you manage to get by working or . . .?*
LB It depends, sometimes I'll work, and I won't go out for a couple of weeks and I can work really hard during that, 'cos like I'm still signing on. I shouldn't be, 'cos occasionally I get work – I'm working all the time – but usually you just break even in the long run, but sometimes I'll get a couple of hundred pounds and I'll spend it on this place but it goes quickly enough. I haven't been on a holiday or anything for, I suppose, eighteen months, which isn't really a long time but I would quite like to go away, 'cos that's one thing I like; I really like travelling and seeing new things.

SW *Going back to this place, right where we started from, what sort of atmosphere do you think you're going to try and create here?*
LB Well, as a joke we've told everyone we've moved into our luxury apartment and we started looking at carpets. We saw this gross shag pile but it was dreadfully expensive, it was eight pounds a metre or something a square foot – some ridiculous price – so we got the next that we found: a really beautiful fun fur which has black roots and silver ends which is really long and I can do the whole flat for a hundred pounds, I mean every room, and I even made allowances for my bedroom walls as well, so that's much cheaper, but it

will give a very luxurious though a bit horrible, I mean like a send up of a luxurious flat, I do want to be comfortable at the same time so, 'cos I get, I do get a strong feeling from wherever I am, sort of the environment I'm in, if it's comfortable I can work here, like it's all the better for me.

SW *So it's got to have a dualistic function because it's for working and living in?*
LB Well, I don't really see the difference, I mean I work all the time, even when I'm just sitting down watching television. I don't sit and watch television that often, but I'll always be stitching something even if it's something I'm going to wear that night. I don't see the big definition between work and living.

SW *But it reinforces the separation between the inside and outside?*
LB Yes, definitely. Once we're in, we're really in, like everything's shut outside us. We're eleven stories up; we can look down on everything and say, 'We're quite safe, feel quite safe from this position', and the more we do to it the more it seems almost like a classic escape but, I don't know, it's just an environment where I can feel really happy to be in, it helps me, my ideas keep ticking over, and I want to work here and keep doing things.

SW *You don't feel isolated being in a tower block?*
LB No, I don't, I quite like that feeling of being away from everywhere else but still being able to look down on it, as though we're like a space ship or something just hovering above everything.

SW *You don't feel like physically or psychologically distant from the ground or anything like that?*
LB When I painted the windows I opened them up and looked down; it was broad daylight and it's eleven stories up. It's a really long distance and when we first got here we went out on the balcony and we were spitting to see how long it would take to get down.

SW *What pressures do you . . .?*

LB Well, I've never got enough money to do, you know, all the things I want to do, but that's good in a way because I actually become resourceful. Like, for example, that shag pile, we're going to replace it with something even better, like this beautiful fun fur.

SW *I suppose we're talking about aggravation from neighbours and things but do you get any general aggravation from people?*
LB Oh, you get ups and downs, I mean, it happens all the time, I'm always meeting people as well, because of the way I look people come up to me, so you quickly learn what people are like, what you're going to expect from them and what they'll expect from you and so you can handle things like that quite easily.

16 April 1984

SW *Right, these are just some questions that emerged from looking at the transcripts of the first tape we made together. One of the things that interested me was whether you felt that these days the only way to get a place like you've got is to do something fairly desperate, you know, that's the only way you can get something out of the council?*
LB I suppose you do get it if you're prepared to wait, but we weren't, we just wanted it straight away. We're always a bit eager to get things done like red tape and things like that is pointless, so we tried to think of the fastest way we could, like burning our front door down and pretending we were being harassed all the time.

SW *Now you're in here, are you trying to create a special atmosphere inside the place?*
LB Well, I suppose, because the government and society's got those sort of priorities, yes, I do want to create something where you can think the way I do that's completely separate from it, you know, in a way a bit like an escape from all the pressures I normally feel, like when I turn the TV on I see them again, but the environment's a bit like a capsule or something; sort of separate.

SW *Do you feel free here to do the things you want to do?*

LB Well, I always need to find some way of expressing ideas I've got, and sort of decorating this, and like I've got an environment I feel happy in. It's just one way of doing that, so it doesn't have to be the way this flat's decorated to express yourself, but in my case, it's a good form of expression.

SW *And one thing that really interested me – for symbolic reasons in my work – is the difference between inside and outside the flat. You say you can express your own sensibility here, but do you find outside is threatening in some way, when you look out of the window?*

LB Well, when you're on the eleventh floor it's like looking at things through a microscope and it doesn't seem like a threat or it seems like you're completely separate, like lifted above it, so it doesn't bother me, and I never think of it. Downstairs don't seem the same as up here, it's a different building outside, up here.

SW *Even when you just get in your front door?*

LB Yes, it seems like the lift transports us into where we're safe and happy again.

SW *So as soon as you even just leave the lift door you're feeling. . .?*

LB I'm definitely not very comfortable in the lift, sometimes I don't want to see my neighbours either; I've only seen them a couple of times but I don't really want to be friends or anything with them, I'm sure. I've seen them a couple of times and I don't seem to have much in common with them, I just want to get in here and just shut the door behind me.

SW *But do you see society generally as made up of aggressive forces?*

LB I think they use aggression to perhaps squash people if they say, 'I don't believe that things should be run that way', they'll use aggression to keep you quiet.

SW *Yes, but do you ever feel personally threatened?*

LB Like when I'm dressed up. Yesterday, for example, we caught a bus at eight o'clock and it was still light and the local kids were out playing and they followed us all to the bus stop and when we got on the bus they started throwing cans at us. I wasn't really threatened, or thought, 'Oh, my life's likely to be over', but at the same time it wasn't pleasant.

SW *Do you see the club as a capsule in a way then, as if it was equivalent to almost being here?*

LB That's right, I mean we'd get dressed at home and the journey, unless it was in a taxi, wouldn't be that pleasant and then we'd get there and be happy and comfortable again, enjoying ourselves.

SW *But in those days you weren't wearing such extreme clothes?*

LB No, but I still felt comfortable there and the sort of things I was wearing were appropriate to what most people were wearing in the club.

SW *You say that people can draw something from your personality by what you wear. What do you think people's reactions are, what would you like them to think about you when you're dressed up?*

LB I'd like them to think: 'Oh look, there's someone different'. I'd like them to say, 'Oh they're dressed like an Indian God, but then they've sort of got these 1970s platform things on', and then they'd think 'He's wearing something that's satin, but he's got a big piece a plastic cut in it as well'. I want them to start thinking why I'm dressed like that, why is he using such, diverse things, what's he trying to get at, where does he want to go, and just sort of ask questions and, why should I look the way I do, I mean, 'Should I feel threatened because he looks different?'

SW *Yes, it's interesting, Are you interested in objects. What objects would you like to possess?*

LB Well, the only objects I like are soft, sort of soft-centred ones like shoes, pieces of jewellery. I used to collect vases and things, but because I'm so into my appearance all the time they seem a bit superfluous, so I stick with things I can use, like plates and cups and things that I use all the time. I'm quite into them because I see them or I like them to be pleasing to me. We're going to get this china, just plain white china from Woolworths and you can buy these dyes and things you paint on to it, leave them to dry for forty-eight hours or something in an airing cupboard and the design stays on. They'll be quite nice objects to look at and I'll be using them all the time, but objects like – oh I can't imagine – oh it's just the objects that which are immediately around me that interest me.

SW *So objects are like tools that you need?*
LB I do like having nice tools, the standard of my work's better when I've got the proper things to use. I like my machines when they're running smoothly and I've got a good stitch: that is really pleasing. Once upon a time I couldn't care less, but now I feel really happy when they're working, 'cos that's all buggered up at the moment.

SW *Finally, does being poor at the moment, make you even more creative and more ingenious?*
LB Maybe more resourceful. If I had more money I'm sure I could do even more, but this way, the options aren't so great and so I suppose resourcefulness is a sign of the times as well, when you have to. For us it's how I wanted to use shag pile carpet, but instead we're using the cheapest fun fur I can get, but I think the effect will be more interesting and also, perhaps it says something about the time I bought it.

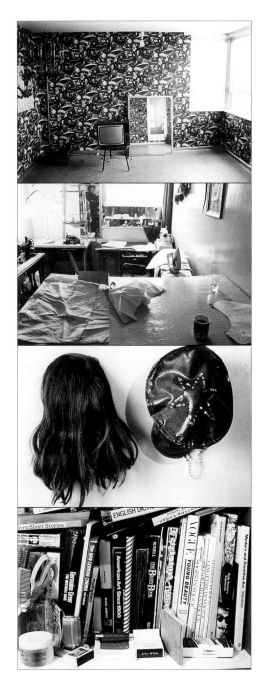

WHAT IS HE TRYING TO GET AT?

ONCE I'M IN, I'M REALLY IN. EVERYTHING'S SHUT OUTSIDE. I CAN LOOK DOWN AND SAY I'M QUITE SAFE IN THIS POSITION, AS THOUGH I'M IN A SPACE-SHIP OR SOMETHING, JUST HOVERING ABOVE EVERYTHING.

What Is He Trying To Get At? Where Does He Want To Go?, *February/July 1984, two panel work with breeze block column, 152cm high by 98cm wide, ten blocks 44cm wide by 20cm high. Photographic prints, photographic dye, acrylic paint, Letraset text, felt-tip pen and objects given by Leigh, on paper and card*

I SUPPOSE IT'S LIKE SORT OF ADVOCATING TOLERANCE, YOU KNOW, DON'T CRITICIZE OR BE HOSTILE TO ANYTHING THAT'S DIFFERENT OR UNUSUAL OR SOMETHING THAT YOU'RE NOT FAMILIAR WITH.

WHERE DOES HE WANT TO GO?

Difficult Boy in a Concrete Block

A capsulised world is created within the domestic space by objects used to construct a display, and which denote a self-image to the possessor, which reflects his or her self-organisation and personal sensibility. Against the physical and symbolic mass of modern architecture, the capsulised domestic world lives in an enforced coexistence which parallels everyone's relationship with society – the private, inner self is expected to adapt to, and comply with, a publicly acceptable code of social behaviour. *Difficult Boy in a Concrete Block* is divided between night and day to state clearly what transformation can mean within such an overt symbol of determinism: a council flat inside a twenty-storey concrete tower block. This transformation uses the private world of the flat as a catalyst for the creation of a sensibility that expresses the possibilities of community.

Inside the flat, my work associates the day with the physical determinism represented in the physical mass of the tower block that governs normality, the struggle of everyday existence. The night is then associated with the psychological freedom that is also possible within the very same space, a prerequisite to a counter-culture based on self-organisation. The underlying form of the work stems directly from the contrasts in John's life, a young man who co-operated with me over five months, concentrating the work on his experience of domestic reality within a tower block in North London. Present in this environment, also in a kind of coexistence, which in turn reinforced John's coexistence with the world around and outside him, were objects that expressed different cultural states in his life, and, as day went into night and night into day, so various objects became dominant and important.

John, 7 July 1983

SW *I'm sitting in John's flat, 9A Sandridge Court . . .*
J Queen's Drive.

SW *First of all can you tell me how you came to live in here?*
J I don't know, just by hassling the council really, but its quite good. I applied with this bloke called Matthew and we decided after about six months that we weren't going to live together 'cos we wouldn't get along at all. We argued the whole time but we got a lot of points 'cos it was a joint tenancy plus I got medical reasons which was how I got a lot of points. He got thrown out of the place he was living in, so we told the council that he was sleeping on the sofa where I used to live, which immediately put us up into the emergency housing list. It was all true, but it wasn't really because he didn't really want to move in but he might have done, and then we got it just by hassling, 'cos I said I didn't want to live anywhere else but on this estate, because all the others were really horrible.

SW *What was your first response when you came in here? You're nine stories up, how did you feel like about living up here to start with?*
J Oh, I got vertigo, I was scared, 'cos first of all I was really worried about the cat, 'cos I just thought it would go on the balcony and fall off, but it didn't, and I don't care about it now 'cos I've got used to it. I was really pleased to get the flat, I didn't really care if it had been sort of nineteen floors or one floor I was just going to keep the balcony doors shut the whole time, I was going to lock it or something, but I'm really pleased that there is a balcony I've got used to it, I'm not scared at all.

SW *What was the response from your neighbours, did you have much contact with them?*
J Well, the only thing, the couple next door, and it's quite funny really – the thing is, in these flats there's two bedrooms on the other end, and there's an old couple living on the other end, a young couple live in the middle,

and the old couple thought it was my parent's flat first of all; they thought I'd moved in with my parents. The couple next door thought we had kids 'cos there was me – you haven't met Marion my flatmate – but they thought that sort of we were a couple, you see. They thought, 'How can they have two bedrooms and we've only got one?' They were really upset, they kept asking people in the lift, friends of ours coming up, saying; 'How can they have two bedrooms, have they got kids or something?', you could tell they were really jealous that we've got this two-bedroomed flat and we say it'll serve them right for getting married.

SW Do you gravitate towards the places that have some identity separate from, the normal society in a way, for instance, how do you live, do you have a job or what?
J No, I don't do anything, I mean I get by, just, I don't know . . . I get really broke but I get more fun going out than I do doing anything, 'cos I really like getting pissed out of my head and having a good time and getting off with people and things like that. I think that's got a lot to do with it, the fact that you're queer, you have to go to places that are different, 'cos you are; it's as simple as that, you can't carry on a straight way of life 'cos you don't think like straights. When I say straight, I mean straight as in the straight way of thinking that you have to sort of conform to be able to fit it.

SW Yes, you don't feel like doing something then, like getting a job?
J No, I have no desire to work whatsoever, I just don't want to work. It annoys me that you should have to work to be able to enjoy yourself, I just don't think that people should have to be pushed into it, I think people should just be able to go out. God, you only get one life, and what is the point of wasting it away, you know? I mean I feel really sorry for these people who get married and settle down and have two kids and I just think, 'Well, what the hell's the point?' Okay, they'll probably say the same about me, but I'm sure I have a darn sight more fun than they do.

SW So do you feel alienated from all society generally, when you look out the window and you look down on those houses?
J You know I hate them all, I think that, well, for a start I am different 'cos I fancy blokes, it's completely beyond the majority of the population's comprehension, they don't know what you're talking about, they don't understand that you should have that sort of freedom to be able to do what you want.

SW They really want social conformity?
J Well, yes, I think that's what it is.

SW But you don't want that, do you?
J I don't want anything that's anywhere near that. I like the idea of not being part of society, I have no wish to work at at all, I don't see why I should. Why the hell should I, I'm not going to enjoy it. I'm going to do something that I enjoy then that's not what I'm going to call work, 'cos then it's not work, is it? If you enjoy it, then I don't think you can say it's work, 'cos work is something you have to do to make a living, whereas I think if you're doing something like you're doing, which is something that you really like, it's not really work, well not the straight definition of the term work.

SW Do you feel isolated physically from the ground?
J Yes, I do, I think it's really funny when you go to people's houses on the ground.

SW Do you?
J Yes, Marion went round the other day to her friend's who live in a basement and she was sitting there thinking, 'God, this is really weird', 'cos she was in this basement, and I know exactly what she's talking about. I couldn't imagine ever going back down to live on the ground now, I just wouldn't 'cos it just seems right that you should live this high up. When you go out you go down, it just feels weird, so, I don't know, I can't describe it really, but just going round to people's houses when they're just a floor up or something you think, 'Where's the view?'

SW Do you find people talk to you in the lifts?

J They're a bit scared of me, I think.

SW *Yes?*

J I think they are, yes, 'cos they don't really understand. I think a lot of them are really resentful of the fact that I've got the flat in the first place because in a lot of the blocks in Hackney you do sort of get lots of people like me, 'cos it's quite easy to get flats when you're prepared to take anything, but this particular estate is really popular, it's the most popular estate in Hackney, so obviously there's a hell of a lot more people want to come here and I think they're pretty resentful of the fact I'm in it.

SW *How do you get any money then, to do things?*

J I do actually try and work out where I get money from, but I suppose I scrounge a lot off people and I borrow money. We owe quite a lot of rent but that's no problem, 'cos if you get notice of arrears you just pay it, they don't really care, I mean even if you just pay it once every six months, so long as they get it they're not bothered really, so I don't really care, but the only point of having a flat is so that you can go out and enjoy yourself, that's the whole point of living 'cos it's such a fucking shitty world basically. It's no sort of life for you really, at all, if you just carry on. What I'm supposed to do is go out and get a nine to five job, but if I get a nine to five job I won't have any time to go out in the evenings 'cos I'll be too tired, so I'm just going to end up spending all my money on things like vacuum cleaners and colour TVs, which is a load of crap really. I just don't want it, I'd much rather go out and get pissed every night.

SW *Do you ever think of other people living around you? Do you want to know about them or have anything to do with them?*

J Not particularly, no. I don't really care what they do, I mean their lives have nothing in common with mine, and the only thing – I think I said this before – that they just get really jealous 'cos they can't understand why we've landed this two-bedroomed flat and they haven't. I've got nothing in common with

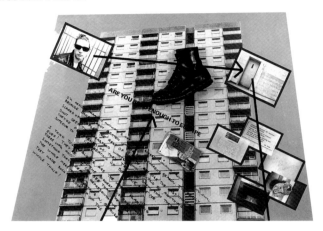

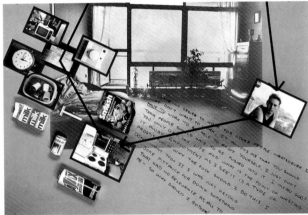

them, how can you, when you meet these people in the lift and you're talking to this woman and, and she's racist and she automatically thinks you are too.

SW Most of the contact you have with people round you is a bit unpleasant then?
J Not unpleasant, not specifically unpleasant to me, but they're just not the sort of people I can be bothered with, you know, they're just naff straight people in my opinion, you know.

SW Do you ever feel frightened by the tower block? Do you ever feel like it's going to fall down or that cracks are going to appear in it?
J No, no, I think it's really exciting. I really like the idea that it might fall down, I do, I get a real kick out of it, it's brilliant.

SW You don't ever feel frightened when the wind blows hard?

J No, I really like it, I'm always hoping it's going to be hit when we have a thunder storm, 'cos you know, I think it would be really brilliant if it got struck by lightening, it would be so exciting and I think it would be a brilliant way to go 'cos I'm not really bothered about dying like that or anything. If ever they drop the bomb I'd say it would be really good to have a party 'cos you can have such a good view from the balcony.

SW Just talking with you, what seems to come out is the role of drugs and things, or dope. Can you elaborate a little bit about the role of that, and getting pissed, sex . . .
J It's just another way of getting out of it really, having a good time.

SW But generally, do you think it just becomes part of the culture?
J Well, I think after a while you realise, 'cos

first of all it's enough just to go out and enjoy yourself and dance and then you realise that you have to get pissed before you enjoy it 'cos it's all got a bit boring and after that you get drugs, you know, like it's just another progression, another step further, which is why so many people end up being junkies, because things get so much for them that they just have to get really, really out of it the whole time.

SW *But is it considered normal within the groups of people that you know?*
J Oh, yes.

SW *Can you elaborate on it a bit, because you talk about that sort of thing really naturally?*
J Well, I never really think about it 'cos it's so much a part of my life. I don't really think about it as being drugs at all, it's just other things, like when you get stoned it's so different to

getting drunk, and then when you take speed that's another different thing again. It's like different forms of getting out of it really, I don't ever think about the connotations behind it.

SW *But you always feel you're in control?*
J Yes, well, I'm more in control when I take drugs than when I get really drunk I suppose, 'cos acid is about the only one you can lose control by. I think you have to be a bit paranoid in the first place to lose control, I mean that's my favourite, I really like that the best.

Difficult Boy in a Concrete Block, *July/November 1983, four panel work, 145cm wide by 96cm high, with tower made from concrete blocks. Photographic prints, photographic dye, acrylic paint, Letraset text, felt-tip pen and objects found by John, mounted on paper and card*

Sitting Between Two Desks

As part of an ongoing series of works started in the 1970s, centring on various polemical issues in contemporary life, I made a group under the heading *Four Professionals* for an exhibition of the same name at the Lisson Gallery in 1980. The works in this group concentrated on the psychological and physical pressures on the individuals who dealt with the distant mediation of large numbers of other people as an aspect of their professional role. A relationship was made, as an active process, between the environment in which decisions were made about others, and the actual effect of those decisions on the context in which people were to be influenced. Works were made with a City banker, a newspaper editor, a curator at the Tate Gallery and an architect.

Sitting Between Two Desks was made with the architect Mike Lynch, who was concerned with the less glamorous end of the profession in the rehabilitation of old buildings up to the 'contemporary standards' of his Housing Association clients. The effects of his decisions played an enormous role in conditioning the future lives of the incoming residents of the rehabilitated buildings.

In developing the work, I set out to uncover how the architects – whom I saw as symbolic of the idea of the 'professional' – constructed a psychologically acceptable relationship between the office environment, its daily reality, and the world of the residents and builders associated with the building. The work is structured as a sequence of four panels that document the process of the work, from the initial conception of a scheme, to its final implementation and habitation. The sequence presents the viewer with an evolving symbolic world, in which four questions are posed as problems to be resolved by making connections between the purposefully disparate references provided. This symbolic world was built up by the architect entering into a co-operation carried out over a year-long period, where a number of documentations were made, photographic and tape-recorded, to base it on his actual experience.

In each panel two objects associated with exchange between the two separated environments are shown in a matrix of visual and textual references. On the one hand this shows the determinism of the position the professional decision maker is trapped within, while on the other it displays the self-organisation manifest in that situation, to express the personal psychology and creativity of the individual.

Mike Lynch, 28 May 1980

SW First of all I would just like you to very simply describe what your work involves. What do you do?

ML Well, officially I am a job architect for the practice, leading a team of architects doing a housing programme, primarily for one large client. In this case it's the Notting Hill Housing Trust, and they have an ongoing programme of rehabilitation in and around Notting Hill, nearly all 'rehab' work and a small amount of new building. The housing trust is funded by central government through various channels, so the money is really public money and that actually influences what we do. My job is to take the original brief that we get from the client – they will give an address of a house that needs to be rehab'ed which they own or are about to buy, together with an indication of the sort of mix they want to get into it – and I then organise from this office the fulfilment of that brief.

SW You have a very particular working environment, haven't you? Can you describe it for me? What can you see from your desk?

ML Well, it's special in that it's quite new. We recently had this extension built on to the back of the building that we own. It's a large, open-plan drawing office and we specifically designed it this way to get cross-referencing between people. So it's a large, open, carpeted space, glazed fully at one end and opening on to a very nice garden with trees, There's a series of drawing boards set around with layout spaces, groups of telephones, groups of filing cabinets close to each work station. It's a well-lit, ceiling-heated building, fairly high technology in that respect, which in my view is quite successful, but in fact is not liked by a lot of people that work in the team. It's visually very pleasant for visitors coming in, most visitors are fairly impressed. It's a nice-looking place but it has some drawbacks in terms of working. There is sometimes too much cross-referencing going on.

SW You hear a lot of noise going on?

ML You hear a lot of noise, it can be a problem if you're on the telephone and someone else is talking very loudly or playing the radio or just talking about something which you find irritating or boring or whatever; that can be a bloody nuisance.

SW So do you think there is a relationship between the bureaucracy of your work and the creative element – or do you see a sort of separation there?

ML Less and less. I must say that the administrative side of getting a house rehab'ed is enormous, the amount of administration that goes on really is incredible, and most of my time is spent in answering letters dealing with the housing corporation, the department of the environment: dealing with the petty bureaucracy that absolutely envelopes you. The amount of time that we actually spend consciously thinking that we are doing something creative is fairly small. I don't think I consciously think of it, apart from the initial feasibility study when I am looking at a plan and thinking, 'Well, what's it going to be like to live in here – how would I like to live in this flat?' The people who we design for – what sort of lifestyles have they got, how will it work in this plan, on a very sort of detailed basis? Are they going to want an opening between the living room and the kitchen or are they going to want a door to keep the smells out? Do they want a big living room and a small hall, or smaller living room and large hall that they could furnish, because many of these people are coming from old accommodation with big heavy furniture. You've got to think about that, I mean it's important that they keep their lifetime possessions and you have to think of those things and in some way that's, I don't know that I would call it creative, but it's sort of creative, in that you are creating an environment in which they are going to live. You think consciously about it.

SW So you do get satisfaction when you . . . a definite reward?

ML Oh yes, you do, and I think more so when you go back to do your six-month maintenance inspection – it's contracted that you have to do that – and people are actually living in there and then you can see what they have done. It's interesting just to see the way they have furnished it, put their own wallpaper up, curtains or whatever. In some instances they've tried to make radical changes and you realise you were possibly wrong in your concept of what should be in this building.

SW Do you ever become conscious of the fact that, sitting in this office at that drawing table, these designs are actually going to be realised in a physical way?
ML Yes I am very conscious of that. I think it's almost an aggressive thing somehow to say 'Okay, we are going to plan this building this way'. You can't really avoid that very often, but then you say, 'Okay, we are going to colour it this way, we are going to put this sort of wallpaper up, we are going to put that sort of carpeting down', and you're using your own judgements of what a nice environment is, and that may not be the correct thing to do at all, I don't know. More and more I tend – apart from the planning aspect – to be fairly bland with the flats. I have reached the stage now where I have gone full circle – I paint everything white inside, for example, and in the common areas – the entrance halls and staircases, where things have to stand some hard wear – I tend to play it all down in terms of colour and tone, because I feel it's rather aggressive to impose my feelings on other people.

SW Do you ever get to know the tenants living there?
ML Yes, we do. We often meet them before the building is vacated, when it's in its old state, and we meet up with them again when they move back in or when they move into other property. We keep in touch with them and occasionally meet them in the street two or three years after they have moved in and they tell us what they feel about the building. It's all on a very casual basis, we don't programme it but we do hopefully learn from the comments that people make.

SW I notice just from this conversation that you are of course in a fundamentally triangular relationship – the client, you, and the tenants or the people that are going to occupy these flats. Do you get a lot of pressure from your clients that goes against your own sort of feelings and ideas about . . .?
ML No, I think the tenants have the least pressure on us. I'm not saying that that's the way it should be, maybe the tenants should have the greatest pressure on you as they are going to live in there, but from a practical point of view until the building is handed over, often nobody knows who the tenants are going to be. When we know the tenant is going to move back in, the client will often ask us to liaise with that tenant who might have some extremely strange ideas which go very much against the grain. You really have to remind yourself of this feeling of arrogance that you might have, and you've got to say 'Oh well, maybe it's a stupid idea you know, oh Christ, I don't know how you could possibly live in there', or even, 'What happens if this guy moves out – who the hell else could ever live in a place like that?' If he moves out after six months, a lot of money and effort has been put into a flat that nobody else would go near, but they do have a right to say the sort of environment they want to live in, and we listen to them but that doesn't often happen.

SW What are the major problem areas in this relationship with the client? Speed . . . time?
ML Speed is one thing, but often you work best under pressure anyway – I think lots of people do, so although it's a pressure, one that I wouldn't argue with, it's okay. The big problem is having to cope with this continual problem of finance, trying to produce a building which is pleasant to live in and has some beneficial effect on the overall environment; in other words trying to persuade the client that it's important to spend money on the outside of the building, on nice railings and things for the benefit of other people living in the street who are not the client's tenants.

SW What kind of pressures build up on you generally within your work? Where do they come from?

ML The pressures come from the deadlines that have to be met, either in getting a job to the client in the initial feasibility stage or in meeting the deadlines that the contractor requires. Contractors require certain information by certain dates: if they don't get it they can bypass the client and clobber the architect. If it's shown that we were either negligent or just slow, the client can come back and we have to basically pay for it either in cash terms or in not getting any more work.

SW *Do you sometimes feel that you are under stress?*
ML Yes I do, yes, I feel that I am under stress sometimes, although that feeling of stress, funnily enough, I feel that I can cope with it. I very rarely wake up in the early hours of the morning sweating and thinking, 'Christ I haven't done this or I haven't done that'. Occasionally I suddenly remember that I haven't done something very important, but I don't feel that I have a stressful sort of profession and I don't take my worries home or at weekends or things like that.

SW *Are there any inanimate objects that you would associate with this pressure?*
ML I suppose the most obvious one would be the building itself, because there it is when it's finished, £100,000 has been spent on it, for example, it's there for everybody to see and if you have made a cock up, if you've allowed one of the job architects to carry out the most horrific colour scheme on the outside of the building and it stands out dreadfully, then you're stuck with it.

SW *So you have this fantastic sort of social responsibility in a way, don't you?*
ML Well, yes. The social responsibility is on me in that I am the job leader.

SW *Do you feel this public responsibility? Can you describe what it is?*
ML Yes, well, it's a feeling you have – you've been given a property or a house to develop and finish for the people who are going to live in it and those who are going to live around it as well. You have a duty to make it look

correct somehow – it's the other people who live adjacent to it that will see it every day. I don't see it every day once I've finished with it – I might not see it again for six months, if at all – so my feelings say I've got to do something which is satisfactory for them as well.

SW *What kind of values do you think you're introducing to the tenants of your rehab'ed houses, just by physically dividing up the space priorities?*

ML I think you're in a position of being able to show the people coming into the property that here is a new flat. It's a new way of living for them, a better way of living. It's going to enhance their lifestyle and allow them to express their own thing, their own feelings or their own idiosyncrasies within their flat. Very often they have come from real slummy dwellings or controlled tenancies where they weren't allowed to do anything at all, and I think that what we try to do is show them a different way and a nicer way to live or a nicer place to live in, and hopefully to make their lives more comfortable and more satisfactory.

SW *But do you think people respond to that? Do you think they do change their attitudes and behaviour as a result of going into a nicer flat as you describe it?*

ML The potential is there for them to do it and I think that in some cases they do, in some cases they don't and in other cases it's very difficult to judge, but I know that in some instances I've been told by tenants, visiting them after six months or so, that they are absolutely delighted and they have gone out and got rid of their old furniture, and bought new furniture and new carpets. Other people feel that something has been imposed on them and they don't like it – they preferred the house in its old condition or their old house, and they are dissatisfied. I think that sense of dissatisfaction sometimes disappears over a period of three or four years or maybe longer, and they come round to accepting it, possibly subconsciously or without telling anybody that they actually like it.

SW *A lot of people do say that one of the*

problems of modern housing is that people are isolated from each other. I just wondered if you felt that any of those problems were associated with your work?

ML Well I've got a fairly short period of time after completion of the property to get to know the tenants. They are very often strangers to each other they've all just moved into this newly converted or newly built house full of flats, and it takes a long time for them to get to know each other. Quite often in that period they do feel a bit isolated and sort of in a strange place and that takes different people different lengths of time to overcome.

SW *Just switching direction, can you tell me what sort of activities do you engage in to relieve the pressure of work?*

ML I think that one of the pressures I didn't mention immediately is the actual sameness of getting a new commission; thinking to yourself, 'Oh God, here we go again, it's going to be the same old problem'. That happens a lot, you get lots of new commissions because there are lots of small jobs. I think one of the ways this is relieved in the office is the fact that it's a very casual atmosphere, very low-key and laid back. It's not terribly stiff at all or formal, and this sort of casualness – with radios going and people chatting and wandering off into the garden when they get a bit fed up, not having strict hours to keep – helps very much; in other words, when you don't feel up to working, you don't! But if a job needs to be done by a certain time, you work back that night and do it. To relieve the so-called pressures I think there is an overall feeling of casualness and pleasantness that's allowed to prevail in the office, and that's the thing that relieves it.

SW *But don't you do more than that though, don't you have organised teams of cricket and darts?*

ML Oh yes, well, I think all this organised sport thing stems from what I have just been saying. The casual niceness of the office actually prompts people to socially engage with each other. In fact it's slightly more formalised in that we have table tennis for

example on the top floor, we have darts
matches in local pubs, there is cricket in the
summer and the occasional football match. A
lot of the guys in the office get together and
play squash fairly regularly, a few of us play
golf and, you know, a few beers at lunchtime,
not much drinking in the evening – very little
actually – but I think that those social activities stem from the niceness of the office.

SW *Are you ever aware, when you go into
work that you are entering a particular kind of
reality that's somehow separate from the
reality around it, that you're going into a
particular kind of environment?*
ML Yeah, I think that you do. As I'm driving to
work, for instance, I'm thinking about what I'm
going to do when I get there and I'm one sort
of person, and then I park the car and go
through the door and it's like going into a
workshop if you like, there's all your things
around you, all the instruments and all the
necessary books and bits of paper you need
to do the job, and so you're immediately in a
different environment and it's a very particular
one. It's a work environment, there's no
question that it's an extension of the work
outside or an extension of your home. You go
in there, take your coat off or roll your sleeves
up or whatever, and you sit down. You know
that you're in a work environment and from
that point of view it's different from anything
else, and you actually change and you
become what you professionally are.

SW *Are you aware of a difference between
yourself and, shall we say, the people living in
your houses, I mean, is there a difference in
your lifestyles?*
ML I think there is. I find it very difficult to
describe exactly what it is, but I live in a large
block of flats, a mansion block of flats and I
don't know that there are any other architects
in that particular block. I don't think that there
are, but I see all these people going off to
work in the mornings and coming back at
nights, and I see them at the weekends and a
few of them socially. I feel that my job and the
way I do it and the way I'm allowed to do it
influence my life generally, so I feel that I'm

more casual. I feel that I'm less restrained than they may well be – they seem to have much more rigid roles in their lives.

SW *Are these your tenants?*
ML No, no these are people I'm living with.

SW *Oh, I see, yes.*
ML And the same thing goes for tenants, I find that people seem to have jobs which have narrower fields to them and they're therefore much more rigidly controlled by the work they do. They always dress in the same way; every day they go to work in a suit or a boiler suit or they're always wearing a uniform, and I don't. I vary my days all the time and I think my mental outlook probably varies as well, so I feel that, in that respect, being an architect is different from almost any other profession. I feel that the scope of work is wider than a doctor for example, I mean, it sounds like a strange thing to say, but doctors seem to do more or less the same sort of thing everyday. A general practitioner for example, although he's got a very varied job, and the same thing goes for lots of others. I feel that my job is a bit different from theirs.

SW *And what kinds of things do you say to the tenants then when you see them? How would you present yourself to them?*
ML Well, the type of tenants, the type of people that we're dealing with, to begin with, are people who are going to be moved from their present accommodation to a new house, very often not their own choice, but one presented to them because of the conditions in which they've often been living for a long, long time, and so they're very frequently worried and concerned about what's going to happen to them. It's a big, big thing in their lives; it's extremely important to them and they're often very insecure because of it. Knowing that, you play a particular role, I suppose, again almost subconsciously and so the attitude you take is one of anything but officialdom. You get rid of any feelings of officialdom and you approach these people on very friendly terms, you must show that you're a competent person so they feel

confident in you, sound like you know what you're talking about; you're not just pulling their legs, giving them any bullshit. You talk very casually, explain things to them in a nice friendly way and react to the sort of people they are.

SW *When you're drawing up these plans you're physically distant from the reality that you're making a drawing about. How do you bridge that physical gap . . . I don't mean actually go there but the moment you're actually sitting down?*
ML Well, I tend to relate the situation to my own life, for example, having talked to a tenant, I might not start that particular project for months, and in the interim all I can remember are certain specifics that they've asked. I've got a picture of the sort of people they are, but it's distant. When I'm doing the work I often relate it to what I would like, and how I would like to live, and hope that's not too aggressive an approach.

SW *But, yes, so, you're working and then you stop work and you're looking out the window . . .*
ML Yeah.

SW *How does it work?*
ML Well, it's a great sort of hotch potch but I think that I very rarely stop and put my pencil down, for example, and stare out of the window to try and get inspiration to do something, or sit there staring out, working out in my mind a plan or plot, it doesn't work that way. When I stop and look out the window – which I do an awful lot – I find myself thinking about all sorts of things, where I'm going to go on holiday, you tend to switch off for a while, rather than actually looking out the window and switching on, you look out the window and you switch off, funnily enough.

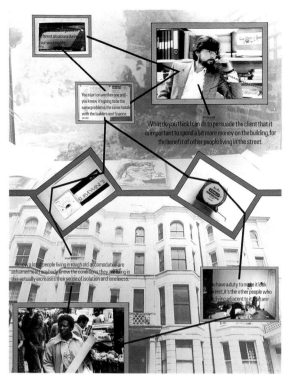

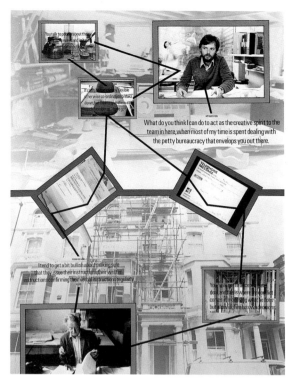

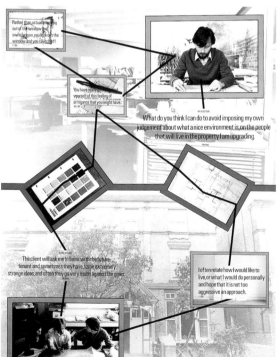

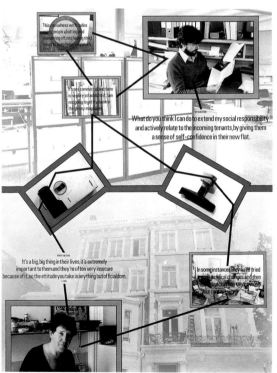

A sequence viewed from above, L to R of Sitting Between Two Desks, That's where the pressures come in trying to persuade them to be a bit more free, *May/August 1980, four panel work, 130cm high by 101cm wide. Photographic prints, photographic dye, gouache, ink and Letraset text, mounted on card*

Inside The Space We Have Been Given

As a critical element in the formulation of a museum presentation of my work, I have often developed pieces which have a special contextual reference to the surrounding area. My strategy is to represent, within the museum, issues that are meaningful to people in the locality, so as to heighten the relevance of the other works and to provide an access for people through the familiar into a territory that they might find normally difficult to enter.

When planning my exhibition at the Van Abbemuseum in Eindhoven (1978), I proposed to create two new works referenced to modern building situations in Eindhoven, as a means of linking works from diverse locations into a central idea that visitors from Eindhoven would already see as meaningful.

One of these new works involved a unique opportunity of working with people who had sole responsibility for allocating council housing in Eindhoven, and as such were at the opposite end of the spectrum from previous installations. The work pressures on Mevr De Vogel and Mevr Pannekoek, housing officers for the Central Woningbeheer Eindhoven, meant that they could only continue for three-month periods at a time. My artwork derived its main focus from this pressure on the two individuals within the confined and deterministic space of the office environment. Interestingly, the 'modern environment' of the flats administered by the two women was mirrored in their office environment, where the same feelings of isolation occurred.

The work is structured over four panels, each dedicated to a particular aspect of the working process in the application procedure, as seen through the eyes of both officers. Objects that are associated with the creation of work pressure are juxtaposed with symbols for relieving that pressure, stating personality and individuality in an otherwise anonymous environment. The resulting work is to be read as a sequence one to four, the process that unfolds typifying office structures more or less everywhere.

Mevr De Vogel and Mevr Pannekoek, 14 May 1979

SW *I wondered if you could just explain, in very simple terms, the overall purpose of the department that you are working for?*
Mevr P We do the assigning of houses and social work – together with two male colleagues. People come here to ask for a house, and we tell them how, when, which house they can get, if they can get a house and how long they will have to wait.

SW *So how many houses do you have in your stock and what sort of turnover is there, I mean, what sort of pressure is there?*
Mevr V Well, we have about 6,000 houses in complexes as we call it, houses in a street, and a changing number – it used to be 1,000, but it is now 500 – of scattered houses, that are houses with ground, or very old houses. This number varies, because it is purchased to be pulled down for new roads and new building projects.
Mevr P And the moment of purchases and demolition is never the same. So these houses are in our hands for a few years – might be one year, might be twenty years – and in the meantime we let it.

SW *So can you describe what the procedure is that someone has to go through to apply for a house, if I was on this side of the desk, as it were? What would I have to do?*
Mevr V That depends, two possibilities, if somebody is a tenant already – in that case he can always apply for an appointment in a letter to talk about his housing problems or application for a house. People who do not rent from us, but from other housing associations, or privately, or people who do not have anything at all, they usually register and at the same time apply for an appointment. They receive an information paper. After a period of five or six weeks they receive a call to come and talk – this is after they have written a letter. There was a time when this period was only one or two weeks, but because of the rush and the shortage we are not able to help so soon.

Mevr P People come to the office more often and the waiting period becomes two months. Talks can only take place twice a year, to prevent too big a rush.

SW *People must get very frustrated when they can only come twice a year.*
Mevr V Yes, but those people have the same question all the time. It happens that a situation changes because of a different job or family circumstances, illness or whatever, but usually they only come to inquire how they are progressing on the waiting list.

SW *Could you describe your job in turn as you said, the procedure, on a daily basis? From the morning . . . ?*
Mevr P We start with coffee . . . We arrive around 8.30 in the office, we like it better this way, to have a chance to talk to each other about the previous day. We have a cup of coffee together. Every day – except Wednesdays – people can phone us about their situation on the waiting list, about a social or medical indication, or if they see a house empty. Twice a week from 10.15 we have consulting hours. One appointment every fifteen minutes. Sometimes we are finished in five minutes, sometimes we spend half an hour. This goes on until lunchtime. We have lunchtime from 12.30 to 1.30, and the afternoons we all have work of our own to do. There are meetings outside the building, visits or letters to write to assignment for people who get a house. All that sort of thing is for the afternoon.

SW *Perhaps could you describe your job?*
Mevr V In general it is the same. I want to add, that all Monday afternoons and almost all of Tuesday is spent on making the agenda, as we call it. Wednesday mornings we have a meeting with the federation of housing associations and we compare our agendas to prevent double assignments. We also discuss the urgent cases like turnings-out, verdicts with division of property and homeless persons. On Fridays I have special consulting hours from 10.30 to 12.30. Then I get calls from people who need more than five minutes

to tell their story. Every second Friday afternoon I talk with one of the representatives of one of our streets – the street committees – to get an idea what is going on there; quarrels between neighbours, someone moving out of one of our houses and that sort of thing. This is more social work, which in fact is the biggest part of our job. The house assignment is only a small part, but it is the eventual result. The bigger the housing shortage, the more social work.

SW *What do you feel about the conditions in which you work – I mean the building?*
Mevr P It seems a very nice building from the outside – it is only five years old – but we have a lack of space. Too many people in only two corridors. Very small rooms; we'd rather have one bigger room for the two of us and a separate consulting room. The rooms here are anything but soundproof. If someone gets emotional or talks loud during consulting hours, everyone can hear it, which of course is a nuisance, particularly in very private stories. What I mind personally is the air conditioning, always too cold. We can never open a window, which would be nice after having had a lot of different people in this room.

SW *Are there any positive sides?*
Mevr P What I also experience as negative, is that in this building it is hard to get to know the people who work in it. One gets in the lift and goes to his own floor and it's very hard to get to know the people. I haven't worked here for long yet. A positive thing is that we have a nice canteen on the tenth floor, where you can have a good lunch, no hot meals, but all sorts of soup or croquettes, even better than the town hall has. It looks very nice up there, flowers, well-dressed waitresses. On that floor there is also a big room for receptions and parties. Also very nice.

SW *But you have lots of plants. Did you bring these in yourself?*
Mevr V Yes, we bring them ourselves, it needs something, this empty hollow room. Look around in my room; pages of a calendar

to cheer it up a bit. These rooms are like white coffins. It is said that an office should be white and clean, but where I spend a big part of my life I want more warmth. We want to make it a bit more homelike – that is also nice for the people we receive. We are no robots, no machines; we have to do with people. The human aspect is a big thing in this department, which we think is right.

SW *Can you describe the points of contact you have with other colleagues, Points in the work itself?*
Mevr P Actually we have contacts in any point; we learned in this work not only to discuss the pure business matters with the other departments, but to give full background details whenever we can, for instance, when a rent payment is bad, they come and ask us to visit those tenants. Then we don't come back with a straight answer like 'something wrong' or 'nothing wrong', but we give a full report on the visit, our experience, what we felt. The other departments do the same.

SW *Can you describe the typical office procedures that you have to process an applicant for a house?*
Mevr P Someone comes to the office and puts down his name by filling in a form at the cashier's; he gets an information paper, which says that one should apply for a talk by letter, then he gets a call for an appointment. We look over the possibilities, what the problem is, and if he can be helped sooner, because of a social or medical urgency.

SW *Can you describe a typical interview, what sort of things are said – how do you proceed?*
Mevr P That is very personal. Name and information are on the form. Only which district and what sort of house is wanted, and we tell them the possibilities. Very different from one case to another.

SW *How would you resolve a difference of opinion between an applicant and yourself, or one in the office itself?*
Mevr V By talking about it – we keep on

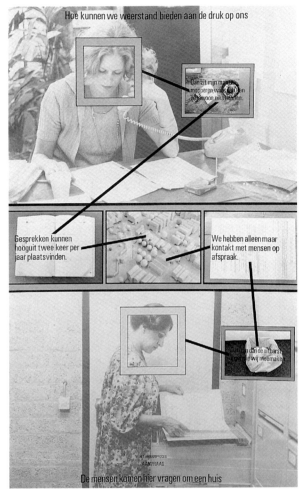

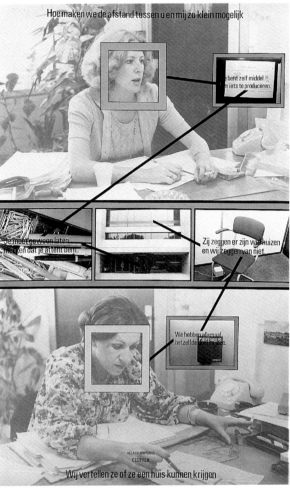

talking till you make it clear that there is no need for a difference of opinion, because there are no possibilities. That is always the problem. The difference is, they say there are houses and we deny that.

Mevr P Yes, we do have differences of opinion in the office, but by talking about it we always try and manage to get out.

SW Do you feel that in the daily work you feel conscious of a psychological pressure?
Mevr P Yes, the pressure is very big. You can compare it with something under high voltage, and where every now and then the fuses go. There are the explosions we go through, sometimes physical attacks.

SW Do you feel that this pressure affects your everyday behaviour in a way?
Mevr V Perhaps not personally, but our environment is certainly affected. If I come home after a tiring week to have a weekend at home, my husband notices that I am very touchy. The best thing for me to do is to sit in a chair, feet on the table, read a book or watch television, I just can't do more.

SW Can you describe the key objects that you consider important to your job?
Mevr V The telephone is one of the most important things, then the desk, but I am not so positive about that, because it is very static. Especially when you have a very personal conversation with people it is better

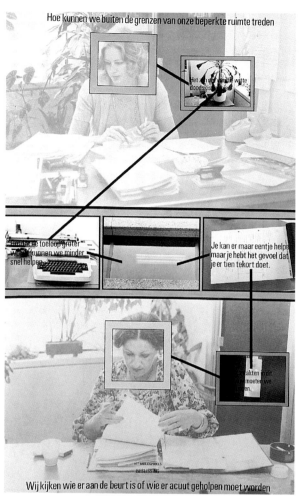

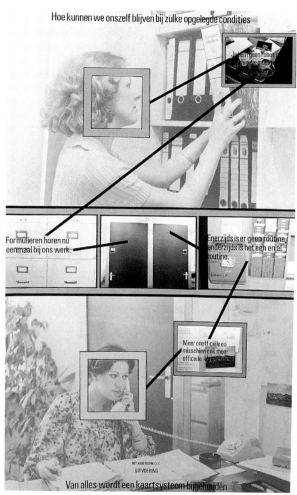

to have a table. If we had a bigger room, I'd put a table with some comfortable chairs to talk, that is much more personal. Another important thing is your pen; you notice that when you've run out of ink, you've got to be able to write. And paper of course. For the rest your own person is very important, you yourself are the means of production; all the other things are of less importance.

SW Are there any more things?
Mevr V In fact this is it, your attitude, the way you sit there and listen. You yourself are the most important, you need to show that you are clear in what you are saying.

SW But you did say that you wanted to change the environment that you worked in, in a way that you felt that it was very small and claustrophobic? How do you think that changing this environment would affect your relationship to people around you?
Mevr P I think it would make it a bit easier, but I also think that it would put people off, they expect to come to a desk.
Mevr V It might work positively, but also very negatively. But that is the same situation as it is now – some find it positive, some negative.

Binnen de ruimte die ons gegeven is, *(Inside the space we have been given) 1978, four panel work, 121cm high by 75cm wide. Photographic prints, photographic dye, gouache, ink and Letraset text, mounted on card*

Sorting Out Other People's Lives

As a contained environment purposefully isolated within society's fabric, the council housing estate represents a powerful context for generating counter-perceptions of the surrounding institutions on which life has been made dependent. Despite the pressure transmitted from such surroundings to remain passive and to separate oneself from others, formal and informal social networks are established by residents. These networks are mechanisms for overcoming the problems of deprivation and institutional dependency. One of the principal functions of such mechanisms is as a means of interacting with an authoritative bureaucracy. Residents in a situation of extreme deficiency and isolation produce their own spokesperson who acts as a catalyst for that community. Such people become reference points within estate life, being principal agents in establishing and running various forms of community facilities. In a sense, the internal fabric of estate life can be seen at a symbolic level as a self-organising system, with the established community mechanisms having the function of maintaining internal coherency.

The Ocean Estate, just off the Mile End Road in London's East End, is a strong symbolic manifestation of a contained environment; isolated and deprived. I therefore identified it as an appropriate context for the formulation of the work *Sorting Out Other People's Lives*. This work centres on Kit Stone, a woman (symbolically representing the individual) who, in her daily life, fulfils various community functions, centred around herself as leader and reference point. A study was made of two fundamental positions the subject occupied within the fabric of estate life: her life at home as a mother, and her role in various community organisations. Four areas of reality were defined within the subject's family life: home, education, economic and social, each matched against a corresponding sequence of organisations in which she involved herself: a tenants' association, claimants' union, a furniture workshop and the Citizens' Advice Bureau.

Kit, who has lived in East London all her life, moved on to the estate to a typical London County Council pre-war terraced block of flats. While she brought up a family of six boys, with her husband unable to work through illness, she was still able to fully engage in the running of four community organisations.

The Ocean Estate resembles a huge transit camp, with many different ethnic groups, ranging from Greeks to Bengalis. Started just after the war, the estate is now one of the largest of its kind anywhere, its expansion matched only by the shrinking employment opportunities. With the local docks and warehouses closing, the main source for jobs has gone, leaving employment now at approximately twenty-five per cent. Most of the residents I met were simply waiting to transfer elsewhere, usually a new town such as Harlow or Basildon. There was very little of the community spirit traditionally associated with East

London. However, there was a sense of community manifested through the consciousness generated by those such as Kit, who refuse to remain passive, and actively set up their own mechanisms. The community organisations have different, though in some areas, overlapping roles within the fabric of the estate. For example, although the tenants' association is directly concerned with the physical condition of the estate, as well as with the establishing of resources there, the claimants' union was set up to help people claim their entitlement from the institutional state bureaucracy, thus also contributing to the general welfare of estate life. In this respect the furniture workshop is particularly interesting, as it was established as a job creation scheme to relieve the unemployment of school leavers.

In the work Kit Stone is viewed as a symbol of all those who actively create a participatory consciousness that counters the institutional pressure around them, which would normally create a conforming passivity. The work was formulated from a number of tape recordings and photographs taken over an extended period with Kit and her husband John. At the start of the process I concentrated on perceptions and attitudes about home life and the estate environment, and this was then used as a basis to view the subject's involvement with the four organisations. She fully participated in the making of the documentations, rooting the work in her particular reality. Thus all the work's visual cues and texts derive directly from the documentations: the loading of the two concept frames associated with each state, contrast the subject's inner reality of the home with the wider reality of her active involvement in community life.

Kit and John Stone, 23 July 1978

SW Well, it's Sunday afternoon in Weddell House on the Ocean Estate. I have to just ask a couple of questions about the sort of environment and how you see it. Can you first of all describe the flat?

KS It's a ground floor flat; four bedrooms, very tiny kitchen and a living room with an exceptionally long passage.

SW Well, that connects up all the . . .

KS It connects up all the rooms but it's a passage that you can't play in. Some flats on the Ocean have big passages you can play in, but this you can only walk in. It's nice but it isn't made for a large family that has to play.

SW How big is the kitchen then?

KS The kitchen you can only stand up in. You can't have a drop-down cooking oven because you can't stand in front of it. I relieved this by taking out all the cupboards and put wall units up without permission. But you still can't put a table in there.

JS You couldn't sit in the scullery with a table and chairs.

SW So where do you have your meals then?

KS In the living room on the coffee table, or on your lap, which doesn't make very good training for children.

SW You haven't got a table you can sit at?

KS No, we haven't got a table in the house at all, because we haven't got room for one, therefore you know it doesn't make good training for children, and it does mean you are continually shouting and screaming, 'Don't drop that on the floor', which doesn't happen in the kitchen with lino on it – you wouldn't worry about it, just get the old mop out and wish wash.

SW How would you describe the community around you?

KS Well I think I am fortunate because I make community. I am quite prepared to go visiting people, and people come in.

JS It is quite a mixed community in this area.

SW What about your work with the centre, that must involve you with the community anyway?

KS Yes, I'm on one of the tenants' groups and therefore I am involved with the tenants. Some tenants. But then you get some of the community who don't want to know the tenants' association. I am only involved in as far as I try to avert evictions because I think it works out dearer to the rate payer in the long run to evict a person any way because you lose your rates and you never get your rent back off them if you evict, therefore I do quite a bit of that. Whereas, quite a few of the tenants' associations don't approve of that at all.

SW Is it voluntary work?

KS It's all voluntary work. I don't get paid for any of it. I am very interested in the Bengali community here.

SW Do you have much to do with them?

KS Yes, I have quite a bit to do with them. We had Margaret in yesterday. She's a cockney Bengali but we have her in. I've got quite a good liaison with the Bengali community on the estate. I rely on John to be here, I mean if John wasn't here . . .

SW What do you mainly look after?

JS I mainly answer the phone and try to tell people where they can find things and give them phone numbers.

KS And make sure the kids are okay, because – let's be fair about this Steve – you hear of all these good women but you never hear how the family suffer. You've got to remember some days I go out of here say nine o'clock and I often don't walk back in here again till half past ten.

SW So if you were working you couldn't do it?

KS No, I wouldn't on principle. I think a lot of the trouble with kids is that they come home to an empty house and Mum's so busy doing this and doing that, then you find full stop, your kids are in trouble.

SW But if you have a problem in the flat, say something goes wrong, can you reasonably expect to get that sorted out?

JS Well, if it's a broken window or any plumbing you want done, if you send a card in, which is on the back of your rent book, it normally takes about three weeks, but it does get done.

KS But of course, like damp walls that's a different kettle of fish. I mean we've gone to the law centre now.

SW You've got damp, have you?

KS Up there, that end room. My Neville pushed us about it, but it's in the law centre hands. It depends on Frank, what he does about it, as far as I am concerned I've done all I can. I've got a bedroom there, has five air vents in it and we haven't enlarged too much, but he'll reap the benefit of the fighting I have already done.

SW Have there been many changes here?

KS The changes, yes the Bengali community. As one person moves out they put Bengalis in, and this thing that they are not mass-blocking, but they are. Definitely mass-blocking Bengalis. I mean what would you say of Bengal House, how many? Half?

JS I would say . . .

KS I'm not talking about the coloured, I'm talking about the Bengalis, the Asians.

JS I would say about fifty-five per cent.

KS And that is out of a block of ninety and they are mass-blocking. They say they're not but they are. They are doing it on this estate. We do single out the Bengalis, everybody will because they are a community on their own. We've got West Indians, as you probably read in the papers this week about the West Indian family, and they're great friends of ours, actually; Nigerians, a few Pakistanis, we've got quite a community of Turkish Cypriots.

SW Do you have much to do with the neighbours immediately around you?

KS The old lady next door, no, because we've all got skeletons in the cupboard and she asks the kids too many questions. We've all got things you go and do and you shouldn't be doing. And Jean next door, I don't see her very much because she's at her Mum's all

day. The only time I see her is when she suffers from depression, so if she's fed up during the middle of the night she'll knock on my door and I'll go and sit in there for a couple of hours. If they want something they know I'm here, and I'll see, but we all do keep ourselves to ourselves, because nearly everybody in this block is doing something they shouldn't be doing. And you know therefore there are skeletons in the cupboards. But they're a nice block because if you want anything you can go and knock on the door. Everybody knows everybody else exists, and I think if one of them was in a bit of trouble everybody else would muck in and help. If there was a flood or anything like that, all the neighbours would go in but we don't live in each others' pockets, which I think is nicer still.

SW Would you prefer more contact or less?
KS No, I like this block as it is actually, because if there was trouble we would all run and help that one out, and that's nicer than knowing you have neighbours you can moan to, but at the same time you have neighbours that don't want to be too nosy and don't want to sit in your home all day. It's nice they know you're there and we know they're there and if we want anything we can go and ask for it and vice versa. We borrow from them and they borrow from us and things like that. So the spirit is there but it's there in a different way.

SW But going back to the work you do on your own, the CAB for example, you must get a lot of satisfaction out of doing that.
KS Well let's face it you do, when you get hold of it, and it so happens to be a Bengali family at the moment, and at work I was asked to go up there and it was appalling up there. It was three beds stuck together and two cots crammed all in this room – it was appalling, really horrible – we've just secured over £500 for another appeal, two appeals had to be done; we had to go back a second time. And now that family is a nice family because they don't live communally with two or three other families, but you go in there now and you can see that they are trying so hard to pick up off the floor. Oh it was right horrible up there, but

pick them up off the floor a little bit you can see that well, you've not knocked your head against a brick wall. With some families you go and you help them all out, and they come back in six months' time and they're just as bad. But it's nice to see some of them getting on; and I just like it. I do weigh people up, you know, I look at them – I'm called the witch. But I do weigh them up, I think that's probably right, and I'm not book-learnt.

SW Because you've had the actual experience, haven't you?
KS If you have had the experience yourself it's better than book-learnt because book-learnt people aren't always very sympathetic, and John is often sick anyway, so old age grows on us.

August 1978

SW The area I want the work to deal with is how you see the institutions in society. The first thing I thought would be interesting to talk about was your work with both the claimants' union and the CAB. I just wonder if you could tell us something about that?
KS The claimants' union is a group of people, who are all on some sort of supplementary benefit. You always get the hardcore few who turn up every week and you get those that just come for their claim and they vanish. The claimants' union do appeals and industrial appeals, tribunals; ordinary run of the day things. Each union is its own boss but they are affiliated to a federation.

SW So where do you get most of your money from, is it from local councils?
KS Donations – we pass the tin round at each meeting, and also, if people get a lot of back money; if they took an appeal for long-term maintenance and they get about £400 back they're quite pleased and send us a fiver. Now we got quite a few strikes on our hands round here so we put out a striker's leaflet, one striker came up and picked up some of these leaflets.

SW *So in what way do you mainly help them?*
KS Helping them to make their claims.

SW *Individuals come up to you then?*
KS Well we do it round the table; it's an open meeting but we only use first names 'cos, people must remember, it's people's private business. We explain to them how best to claim, what to claim for, 'cos lots of people don't know that if you're on sickness benefit and you're on it for twenty-six weeks you then go on to invalidity benefit and then your wife can go and earn £40. But when you're on sickness benefit your wife can't earn nothing because it comes off the benefit – you can't claim for your wife – but if you are on invalidity benefit, your wife can go and earn £40 a week. You would be amazed the number of people who don't realise this. Little things that people very conveniently forget to tell you. And that's what all claimants' union is about; educating people to their rights.

SW *Are they unemployed, single parent families and things like that?*
KS Basically unemployed, one parent families, old age pensioners, but basically in Tower Hamlets we've got very, very, very low employment. On this estate in the last count it was eighteen per cent, but we just got the summer leavers so that puts it down another two per cent.

SW *So unemployment's just gradually increased on the estate? You must know a lot of these people who come in the claimants' union quite well then?*
KS Well I meet them every day, don't I, you know what I mean? I'm flitting round the estate and I meet these people every day.

SW *Yes, but there must be for you – well not an ideological thing – but something that makes you want to do that work? You must feel something about it?*
KS I just feel that someone's got to tell these people it don't matter how many knock-downs you get, if you don't come up and fight these people, who's going to fight them? I just like to be . . . I'm just one of those people who likes

to fight people and argue with people. If I think I'm right I don't shut up.

SW Yes.

KS I mean it – if I'm not sure I go and find out me rights first and then I go back and argue, but I will argue.

SW Do you think the tenants' association could change life on the estate a great deal?
KS Not a great deal because we got quite a few of these older people who are not interested in the social welfare of people. I've done a few battles lately for people being evicted, and they said, 'Oh, they owed rent and they go off', but may I point out to these people that if we don't stop these evictions, if we can't get round this owing of rent, they're going to be a bigger burden on the rate payer because they've got to go into homeless families accommodation; hotels. That way they'll be a bigger burden on the state, that's the only trouble. I don't think a lot of our people are educated in the best way to deal with people who get evicted. They're not very tolerant of split homes, you know, when the wife gets left with all the arrears and then you find there is an eviction slapped on 'cos there's already a possession order on the house.

SW What do you think the community hall could be like, ideally?
KS I would like to see more facilities for the kids on the estate. Quiet facilities. We've got a chess club started but my kids won't go to it, which is a shame. But you know, chess, dominoes, draughts. And I think they could bring the older person in with the younger person. Especially with chess and draughts, you get an older person playing chess and you get one like David; you'll find they can meet on equal terms. They say the old and the young can't but they can; I've seen it done. I have to take a couple of young kids down to Dame Collet, to the play centre, and the other kids mix in very well, and you can bridge the gap there – the old ones will teach the young ones draughts, dominoes, cribbage, things like that.

SW You'd have to be down there the whole time wouldn't you?
KS Well, you see, I'm on the support of the furniture workshop and that's very necessary. Without a doubt if everything else had to go, I would still stay interested in the old furniture workshop.

SW What's that then?
KS It was JC money. You know, job creation scheme money, it was set up with. They renovate furniture and things like that. It's for kids that haven't been at work or been off work a long while. We started off with four kids and when we had the man round to ask lots of questions – evidently they wanted to know the number of the children, how many kids had left – when we said we had only ever lost one in a year he couldn't believe it.
JS They make complete furniture down there as well as restoring it.
KS They strip it and they make complete furniture. You see you know the job creation is changing over, I don't know actually how . . .

SW Is there a lot of job creation here?
KS Round the area yes, I don't know the fine words of it, but they are going to change to a new scheme and the boys are only going to earn £17.50 a week come September. One of the boys is so interested in the furniture workshop, although he's earning £35 now he is going to stay with us under the new scheme 'cos that's all we're allowed to pay them.

SW £17.50, that's not much.
KS Well now, when I spoke to the kids in Stepney Green School they told me they was offered a job for £17.50, they would tell people to 'Stick it up your arse'. So that's their attitude to that. And this boy is going to stay with us – he is one of the wide boys, he's had a bit of bother, but I think but he's going to stay with us.

A sequence viewed from above, L to R of Sorting Out Other People's Lives, *August/November 1978, four panel work, 103cm high by 78cm wide. Photographic prints, photographic dye, gouache, ink and Letraset text mounted on card*

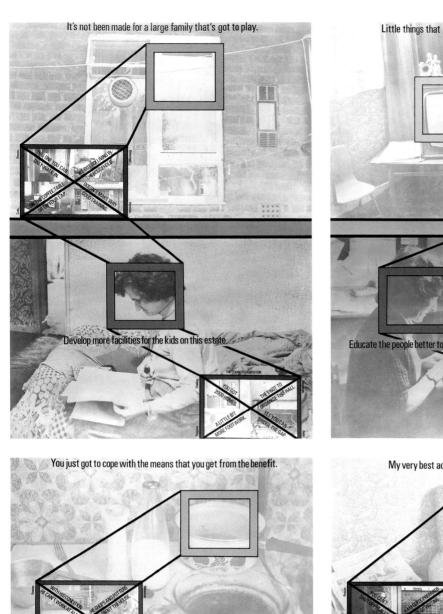

It's not been made for a large family that's got to play.

Develop more facilities for the kids on this estate.

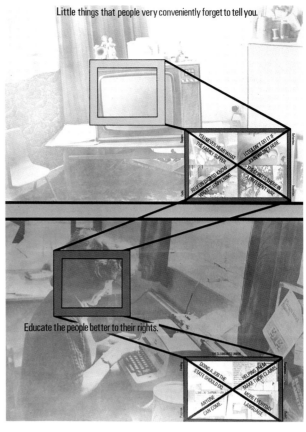

Little things that people very conveniently forget to tell you.

Educate the people better to their rights.

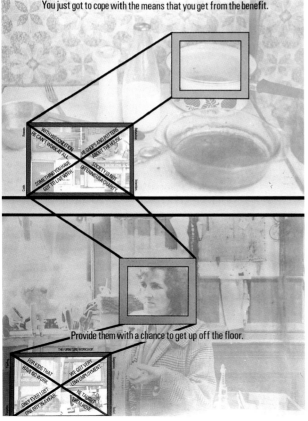

You just got to cope with the means that you get from the benefit.

Provide them with a chance to get up off the floor.

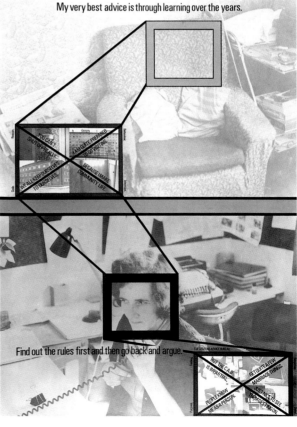

My very best advice is through learning over the years.

Find out the rules first and then go back and argue.

Brentford Towers

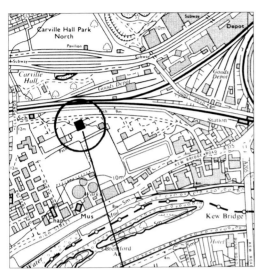

In the conceptual model from which *Brentford Towers* was derived, the tower block is seen as a commonly available symbol that denotes the wider social fabric in which we are all locked. There was a complete binding between the reality embodied in the work, the context in which it was presented, and the primary audience of the work. The work stated a dynamic relationship between the internal reality of life within the tower block, with culturally idealised symbols that featured in the world outside, thus uncovering the means by which residents expressed their resistance to the repressive forces surrounding them in the tower block. The work climbed the inside of the block, floor by floor, to gradually build its own conceptual tower. This made the contrast between residents' possessions (which held a significance for life inside their flat) and objects in the surrounding landscape seen from their living room windows, to which they attached a special meaning. The work was a collaboration between myself and residents of the tower block: I provided the framework while the residents loaded that framework with their own conceptualisations of the relationship between objects on either side of their living room window.

When I first came across the Green Dragon Lane Estate in Brentford, West London, I immediately saw it as a powerful symbol of the new reality. The estate, with its six tower blocks, dated from the late 1960s and, unlike most similar estates, was still intact and operational. Some three months before the work was presented, I selected the middle tower block, Harvey House, as the one in which I would initiate the work. The caretaker, the chief housing officer, and the leader of the tenant's association, were contacted to discuss the idea. I set myself a three week period in which to meet residents, and to discuss with them the possibility of their participation in the work. There would be as many parts to the conceptual tower as the number of residents agreeing to take part during this three week period, each resident making one part of the total model. The tenants' association organised a small meeting for me to talk with several residents, and from this three people agreed to participate, who subsequently introduced me to others. Eventually I gathered together a group of fifteen residents and set about the same procedure with each of them. First of all I photographed, under their control, the objects they considered special to their flat life, followed by objects they identified in the view from their living room window. Next I made a tape recording (later transcribed) in which the resident discussed the relationship between the selected objects. A series of public display boards, assembled from photographs and texts, represented the different aspects of the total model – the conceptual tower – and these were to be positioned on the various landings in Harvey House. Each resident would make one display board from the documentation, selecting the photographs to be used and a quotation from the transcribed recording. This quotation was then written directly on to the display boards by the participant in their own handwriting, the whole display board being made within the same living room represented on the display.

The display boards were presented in sequence, starting from the first floor on 6 October 1985, and moved up with the next display on another landing every two days, until the top (twenty-second) floor of Harvey House was reached. The effect of this presentation sequencing on different floors aimed to change residents' behaviour, so that they would go to floors they would not normally see, and in doing so, meet other residents. The work thus affected life in the tower block, not only conceptually, but also in stimulating new relationships, thus countering the isolating physicality of the block. I asked residents from each floor if they would accept a display board on their landing, and they were only subsequently positioned on a floor when everyone was in agreement. Operation of the work was based on people's acceptance, and it was also important that residents could identify with the conceptualisations made, and for them to recognise the people in the displays, even if only by sight. This

acceptance was demonstrated by the fact that, over the four weeks of the installation, in very vulnerable positions in a volatile environment, not a single display was defaced. The only way the work could be viewed was if people lived in, or travelled to, Harvey House; the actual physicality of the tower was an integral part of the work and had to be experienced first-hand.

John Foster

The following interviews took place in July and August 1985.

SW *The next thing we were photographing and talking about was that radio . . .*

JF The wife bought me that just as I was retiring, so of course I spend the best part of my time out there listening to the wireless while the wife has the television set on. For me, that's my life morning till night when I'm here, listening to the wireless, because I prefer being able to move about and do things during the day, and if I go to the allotment I can take it with me, whereas the wife's got to sit and watch the telly, you can't move when you're watching telly, so I prefer to have the wireless set and move about and do things.

SW *And what about some of these objects here? You've got a great collection.*

JF There is quite a collection there, isn't there, yes, dolls, as I say, a cup there that I had when I was boxing. I was very active, that was when I was twenty, twenty-one years of age. I was very active then, only worked down the Great West Road but I've been in two or three factories there, but of course the boxing club was the main attraction. We do bring back, when we go on our holidays to Spain, we bring back these tiny viewfinder contraptions.

SW *And you've got one for each place you've been to, have you?*

JF That's true, you've got it absolutely, on the dot. Every time we go, whichever place we go to, we bring back one of these viewfinders. Oh the dolls, the wife; most ladies like their dolls, don't they, we brought one or two dolls back.

SW *So mostly they're mementoes to do with experiences?*

JF Of where we go to, yes, in other words getting away from the flat itself, and you've got to bring back a little sort of a memo, to let you know, to remind you of the places that you've been to.

Eileen MacGuire

SW *I'm sitting on the nineteenth floor with Mrs MacGuire in her flat in Harvey House.*

EM Everything is really old, I mean really old, in fact the bedroom stuff I've got there is, is what we had when the war was on, so you can tell, it goes back quite a few years. Never been a one for, well, I won't say that I don't like nice stuff, I'd like it now, but then again I think to myself it's a waste of my money because I shan't be here long enough to see much of it. I look at it this way, because my two children that I've got left, they got lovely homes. I mean, my daughter's got everything; everything's modern and beautiful and all in matching colours. Anything in this house they'd just get dumped – that's why I don't worry about anything in here, but if I knew they was going to say, 'Oh well, I'll have that there', it would be alright.

SW *But everything's got a history to it, then, would you say?*

EM Well, I don't say it has a history to it, but all I know is, it was me and my husband's home and, he's not here and I just like to keep it as it is.

SW *And what about the budgie, you said this was the next most important?*

EM She lets me know there's a knock at the door, and I mean, I've been sitting in here, it's a wonder she hasn't done it now, all of a sudden she'll just go 'whhhsstt', and she'll answer me back like.

SW *So she's like real company?*

EM She is company, oh yes, she is company. See she's doing it again, and even when I go to bed, I turn the light off and she darts down to her seed last thing, as much as to say she's going to go now, I'll have this bit 'cos I won't get anymore till the morning, and I just turn the light off, I say 'Goodnight, Joey,' she goes 'wwhhsstt', just a little, it's funny that, she really is beautiful. Now I know she doesn't make too much noise but she chats, she talks, she says, 'Pretty boy, georgie porgie' and all this, so I talk to her and she sort of answers back, when she feels like it of course, but she is company.

SW *So, when you look out the window do you sometimes feel, I don't know, a bit separated from the world outside up here?*
EM Oh I do because I don't sleep very well and I look out the window and it's all dull, dead. Nothing's moving on the motorway and then there's not much traffic on there really, that I think to myself. I tell you what day I find that it's very lonely and that's Sunday. I always find it's much more lonelier because it's much more quiet. I'm always glad for Monday mornings to come, wherefore when you was at work you'd say, 'Oh, I don't like Mondays'.

Mr Mitchell

SW *Thinking of the principal things that interest you out there . . .*
Mr M Anything, anything in life: it's life isn't it, you're looking at life. You're not as some people in these flats say, 'You're looking at four walls'; you're not looking at four walls, because you've got so much interest round you, always, I mean any time of the day or night even.

SW *What, you see it as like a hubbub of activity?*
Mr M Yes, that's what I say, any time day or night even, I mean some nights you'll hear the old motorbikes, a load of motorbikes ripping up the old M4, well, automatically it's interesting and you're looking at it, or anything like that, or even police cars, it's all activity, isn't it?

SW *But do you feel like the view from the window compensates in a way for . . .*
Mr M For not having a garden? It compensates for not having a garden, point of view, that's the only difference. This is the only thing you miss as such in a flat, the actual little bit of garden, but there's nothing to say you're boxed in because, as I say, really out of twenty-four hours I bet you could get twenty-three hours of interest, you know, that's my opinion.

Marva

SW What have you tried to do in here, because you've done a lot of work on it?
M Just make it cosy. I mean we all sit in here and watch TV, that's the main point, if it wasn't for the TV and the radio, we'd all go mad.

SW So you've got a big video and television, in the centre of the room, can you say a little bit about that, you say it's the centre of life here inside the room?
M Yes it is because it keeps the children amused during the holidays, 'cos as I said they can't go out much to play. While we're in here it keeps them quiet, they watch films and things, though we do go out sometimes.

SW Do they get frustrated, being inside?
M Very frustrated, because they're cooped up all the time unless I take them out, and I can't always take them out 'cos there's things to do.

SW So they can't go out on their own?
M No, it's not safe.

SW Why?
M It isn't, 'cos there's the car park and a few kids have been molested down there, it's not safe to leave them out on their own.

SW The main focus of life in the flat is round the kids then for you?
M Keeping them amused, you know, if I want them happy at the same time, then I can get on with some work.

SW And would you say living in a tower block really did affect your life and relationship with your kids?
M Well, it does, because if you don't go out you don't see anyone obviously, when you do, everyone round here's got children so all you talk about are children. You get a bit cheesed off talking about children all the time.

SW You need a car to travel around but somehow this environment here, it's maybe built for having cars?

M Yes, a lot of car spaces out there, you need a car honestly, 'cos as I say, there's not much in Brentford, there aren't many places for the children to go, they're all outside Brentford, and with three children it's not convenient to lug everything on the bus, so you need a car.

Ken McKay

SW Looking at the way you've arranged that room and this room here, the kitchen, what do you think are important objects that give it that atmosphere you've tried to create?
KM Well, you create it with your own personal touches and I do like plants around the place because living in a high rise block we have no gardens, so I compensate with having plants. I also try to keep an uncluttered view from the windows so we can see through the windows.

SW You think that's important, that sort of contact really, do you miss that at all?
KM Well, not really miss it from the work point of view, but from living in a high up like we do, though I can see more green than most people – living in an ordinary house you can't see the amount of trees and green that I can see from up here – but here there's no way you can touch them as it were, or feel that they're there. They're outside of you, but indoors you can touch them and tend them and all the other things that go with it.

SW In the distance it's almost like a picture.
KM That's right, so to compensate for that I have plants indoors so that we can actually be with them.

SW Well, I'm talking now about the general atmosphere in the tower, has that changed?
KM Well, people would say it has changed, and to a point that's true. When we all came in 1971 we were put in together; it was like a whole host of people all coming and living together and that worked for a little while. Then certain people moved out and others came in, till now there's quite a quite a high percentage of movement, so therefore constant relationships don't get built up as

they used to. When we all came in '71 we seemed to stay together for the first five or six years and nobody moved in and nobody moved out, but now there's been a turn around and because people move out, others move in and consequently you never build up the same relationship again.

SW *So would you say it's very important in tower block life that people are there for long periods of time?*
KM I know others would disagree with you, but they perhaps don't like living here and they've only been put here because they've got nowhere else to go. We've stressed to the council on many occasions that it is an important feature that they shouldn't have these people living in towers that don't want to live here and continue living here. In that way we become a better environment, but to use it as a short-stay place for two or eighteen months or two years is just no good, because that just don't work, because that doesn't tend to build up the relationship within that community or that tower.

SW *Coming back to that room out there, with the television in it, the living room – when you're sitting in there you don't sometimes feel you're in a little capsule do you?*
KM No, no, because I feel I'm living in my sitting room and when I look out I can see the sky and what have you, and if you're living anywhere else you may be able to see across the road to somebody else's house and I feel that's even less of an advantage than I have, at least I have a clear unobstructed view, whereas those others they're just looking out on to a road that does nothing really.

Sharon

SW *You've got quite a few pictures around you, paintings and things like that. Are you interested in paintings or do they remind you of things?*
S Yes, I do, I've got a lot that I haven't got up on the walls 'cos we're saving them, but I do like more modern pictures, got some nice

ones that are put away. I don't like things that are plain; I like a few things hanging about and the one in the hall with the little message on it, I like things like that, just a little sentence that means a lot – that's a little rain in a storm – means a lot, 'cos we've had it hard and it's true, it isn't always easy, you know, as I think just a sentence sums it all up.

SW *But what about the pictures, do they remind you of the outside somehow?*
S Yes, I think so, I mean I love the country and all that, and to look at I think it really puts you into a dream world, because you're in here but you can look at things like that then it's an escapism really. You can look at things and really imagine you're there. When I look out the window it's as though the world's going by without you, you're indoors in here and you look out and see everybody going to work, or some mums walking down the road at half eight and I think, well, I'm still in here and it seems like you're not part of it out there.

SW *Because you're bringing up a family here, this is sort of unusual in this block, a lot of the objects are obviously to do with the children. Do you find you have to have more objects because there isn't a garden?*
S We've always tried to compensate for not having a garden; giving them plenty to do. They do get bored very easy and we've always tried to give them a variation of things as in toys, and also I think my Dad tries to give a lot as well 'cos he knows that they're missing out. They're not any differently behaved, but I still think that you haven't got all the adventures that you would have if you had a garden.

SW *Like building dens?*
S That's it, yes, playing in the dirt and pulling up the flowers and all that, so we do try and provide a lot but I don't know if they appreciate them anymore, but it's there anyway.

SW *Do you sometimes forget about outside when you're in here then?*
S I do, yes. There's been times when I've been in for weeks and weeks and not actually managed to get out, you do, and you're confined really. Although you don't want to be, you end up staying in more and I've hardly really been out at all this year. Before I was always out; you shut yourself in and that's it, I mean it seems such a lot of hassle to go out by the time you've waited for the lift and all that and got outside about four doors, you know; I don't really go out at all.

SW *What about this wonderful machine here, does that somehow replace going out or energy that you might use?*
S I think it is, because I usually get up in the morning, walk down the school, come back and go and pick him up and then that's it for the rest of the day until the weekend, so all I do is my housework, which I can't call exercise. I started putting on weight over the years, well, I was just being a vegetable really, I suppose, sitting in here doing nothing, watching the telly which bored me to tears, so I did get that, now I do five miles a day, or every other day if I'm lazy some days, and it has helped me to become fitter, you know.

SW *What do you do, you just get on that and do five miles pedalling, so what, do you think about something else or what?*
S No, sometimes I imagine I'm going along the road, 'cos I would like to have a go on a bike on the road. I'd be a bit nervous now. I might put on a record or something like that and that sort of helps you do it or watch the telly, you know, but basically I just get on there and I keep looking at the clock to see how far I've got to go, to get on with it. The speedo clocks up the miles and I don't know what I do, I suppose I just sit and think about what I've got to do when I get off it really, start the dinner or whatever, I just get on with it.

SW *Doesn't it occur to you, you know, it seems a bit funny?*
S I did at first, I'm used to it now, yes. I do it in the hall, out of the way, but now I don't care, you know, if someone's here while I'm doing it, I just get on with it, at first I done it in private, and its the same when I'm doing the exercises as well it was all in private, but now I don't care I just do it.

Mr Inman

SW *I'm sitting with Mr Inman, 24 Harvey House. You're living on your own, do you ever feel a bit lonely?*
Mr I No, never feel lonely, no, there's too much to do, cooking, and things like that, and then I get visitors like my son and my daughter. They come round regular, so I'm never lonely up here, never, there's always something to do, washing, things like that.

SW *Do you enjoy doing things like cooking and washing?*
Mr I I do. I've learnt to enjoy it since I've retired, well you get into it I think, it comes natural to you.

SW *What sort of things do you cook then?*
Mr I Well, I don't try out many experiments, just mainly well, puddings I suppose, just frying, chops, don't have chips though, don't like chips.

SW *You don't try anything elaborate?*
Mr I No, you can't really up here, you've got no one to experiment on have you? You've got no cats or dogs to try them with.

SW *You don't ever feel that one day follows another then, like sort of . . .*
Mr I No, every day's different to me. I make it different otherwise you get in that rut you see, you never go out, see what I mean?

SW *So the key to it is actually going out?*
Mr I That's right, and now I've got my bus pass I can go further. Yes, I try and make it different every day.

SW *Oh yes, do you plan it then, do you have to think about it?*
Mr I I don't plan it, no, but for instance, if I go down the shops I go that way one day and I take a different course the next day, see, so it's different, see what I mean? Then I take a few trips up town, you know, see different exhibitions, as I've been telling you, and, I saw the Thames barrier the other week.

Mrs Luddon

SW I'm on the tenth floor of Harvey House and I'm speaking to Mrs Luddon. We were looking at various objects in the flat, and trying to identify those with a special or personal meaning, an association with an everyday routine that you identify with life in the flat. One of the objects was this painting that's above you; can you say a little about what that really means to you?
Mrs L Well, it's a very peaceful picture, it reminds me very much of the village I was brought up in and the happy surroundings that were in that village many years ago. I love green and flowery areas, so that's why I like that picture so much.

SW So, it's really that it reminds you of a past, of a world that you've left behind?
Mrs L Yes indeed, yes indeed, a very happy past. I spent many, many hours walking by this river and the hills as a young girl.

SW Do you sort of daydream?
Mrs L Yes, I do, especially when I'm alone and my family are out. I like looking at it, it's very peaceful.

SW One of the other things you were talking about were the books.
Mrs L Yes, if I'm tense, I like to go into the shelves and find a book for myself and spend a couple of hours reading; that way I'm able to relax and get rid of the tension.

SW What sort of books do you like to read?
Mrs L Any kind of book, I really like to read, autobiographies I like and magazines, *Woman's World*, *She* and *Woman's Weekly*.

SW And would you say that being in the flat here, all made of concrete and high up, that the picture and the books are somehow or other a means of escape in a way?
Mrs L That's quite true, because you're not able to open your door and walk straight out on to the street or out into a park. Yes, the piece of green in my picture and books and records, the other thing is records. I like

opera, yes I do, and country and western, folk, but I have to play my opera records when I'm alone; my family don't like them at all.

SW Now can you tell me a bit about your views from the window, what do you see?
Mrs L I enjoy looking out my kitchen window, it's restful and peaceful to look out over Kew Gardens, the trees and the greenery. And then you're looking down on the river, it's nice to see the boats going up and down and the traffic over Kew Bridge, and then one is able to see the buses going up and down and distinguish the numbers of the buses by the shape of the bus.

SW Do you ever see people from your tower that you don't really know, well, don't know them at all, but somehow you know them from just looking?
Mrs L Yes, you don't know them to speak to but you can, by their walk, and you can just see that figure, but it's from the nineteenth floor it's more visible, but from the twenty-second the figure is smaller because you're so high up. But you can still recognise people at that height, and of course you're used to seeing that particular person.

SW Yes, because maybe they have a certain routine.
Mrs L Yes, a certain routine and you look out and you see that person coming along.

SW So, in a way, there's a correspondence between the picture and some of the things you can see outside.
Mrs L Yes, very much.

SW I was thinking that when you look out, are there any particular things that give you the same impression as the picture, is there a particular view or particular angle or . . .?
Mrs L Yes, looking down on the river and you've got the trees at the back, that is just as that picture is there with the trees at the side and the river running right through, and watching the boats going up and down.

Ron

SW Perhaps it would be an idea really just to start with some of the photographs I took. You said to me previously that you came by these objects, of which there are a lot in this room, not by collecting them but through other means. Can you tell me a little bit about this?
R Well, yes, it's just that a very, very old friend of mine – I don't mean old by age but old in the number of years we've known each other – they actually belong to him and unfortunately he died a few years ago. Thankfully, he left them to me; I think I treasure them more than he does, or did. To me they have, well, they make a very relaxing atmosphere in the room and I look upon it as a sanctuary here, it's my refuge from the cold world outside.

SW But they're very distinctive things aren't they, sort of Chinese figures?
R Well, yes, it has got a sort of oriental flavour. My sister once said when she was up here one evening that, 'cos it was night and when the lights, the lamps are on, the room takes on another character, least I find it so. As I say, I call it a night flat rather than a day one. But to think, as she said, to think you were sitting in a council flat in a high rise block, you know, you would think you were sitting in some luxury block of flats somewhere.

SW So this a sanctuary of memories?
R No, I wouldn't say memories because that indicates that one lives in the past and one lives on memories, and I wouldn't say that at all. It's nice to have memories of course, one's got to be very thankful that one has memories. Again it's one of the things I often say, I think I've had perhaps things many people haven't had, that sort of companionship, that feeling of oneness between two people is something that I think is, I won't say is unique exactly. There's so many married people in the world today living a life together, my experience is that many are very unhappy anyway. It's very difficult to get people to talk about their private lives, their private feelings, relationships they have with other human beings, I suppose I'm pretty reticent about myself.

Mrs Muir

SW I'm up on the twenty-second floor with Mrs Muir. Looking out of the window, what sort of things could you see in the view that were interesting, you mentioned that building?
Mrs M Now that, I always think of sailing, you know, every time, but I think it's because I would like to be on a boat, you see, it's daydreaming again.

SW Yes, that's what I'm wondering.
Mrs M I do like to daydream, oh yes. If you haven't got your dreams, you might just as well . . . because it's the daydreaming you do that sort of keeps you going.

SW So the building – what part of it reminds you of a boat?
Mrs M It's not exactly the building, the actual building itself, its how it sort of forms, I suppose, the roofing and the chimney and all that from a distance in the background. You can only see that part of it along the, what we would call the horizon, it's not that actual building, it's the one right beyond it, and it looks as if you've got the, you know, big funnel and the smaller ones and all different things on it. Actually it reminds me of wartime, like a destroyer, if you can understand the bits and pieces round the side where they've the guns and different things.

SW The other thing you mentioned was the other flats, you know, sometimes you look out and you look into their flats and things.
Mrs M It's just that if you look out the window and the lights are on, I mean I know a lot of people look over to here, 'cos I've actually stood there and watched them, you can see that they're looking over to this part. I've actually seen someone with a pair of binoculars looking, so, it doesn't worry me.

SW You don't shout across to each other?
Mrs M Oh no, no. Half the time I don't think they would hear because right up here when you've got that wind blowing you, know you can't, it's like trying to whistle to somebody down the bottom. You wouldn't get them to hear unless you've got someone with one of those big forcible whistles. The only thing you can do if you know a person you can wave and get them to wave back 'cos sometimes the children might look out the window and see somebody at another window and wave their hand, other than that there's no communication at all.

SW But generally you don't know lots of other people in other blocks?
Mrs M No, no, you only know them by sight, or as you walk past, 'Good morning, Good afternoon, what a nice day', you know, that sort of thing, but you don't know them to talk to, you don't know them personally.

Mr Spiteri

SW If we look around the flat we see that almost everything has been done by yourself. Why do you think you got so interested in DIY?
Mr S I like to make things. I like to see a bit of wood and think, well, that's just a bit of wood and then a couple of hours later, or when you've finished the job, it's something interesting or something useful. Mostly, it's if I get bored, or if I'm watching the television.

SW But you have created a definite atmosphere here, what sort of atmosphere do you think you've tried to get?
Mr S I've tried to make my flat my hobby, I like to make as many things for it as I can, if I see, something in a shop and I think oh, that would look nice in the corner of my flat rather than buy it I'll try and make it first.

SW You taught yourself everything?
Mr S Yes, and then I started to collect as many tools as I could and then about two years ago I got myself a Black & Decker workmate, which has now been stolen. It was down in the shed, somebody stole it, and then about a year ago I got the Black & Decker attachment for making wood dowelling joints and then you can make even better things.

SW Do you feel that growing things has a

particular significance if you live in a tower block?

Mr S Up in a tower block without a garden? I'd have said you're mad 'cos I love gardening and obviously I can't have a garden, so my window box and my house plants is the next best thing. I feed them, I shine their leaves and everything like that and, well, to me they're like kids. Sometimes, my brother'll come up, for instance, and he's got no idea of gardening. He's talking away and the next thinkg is he's dipping his ash in one of my plants, and as you can see I've got hundreds of ashtrays round my flat, and I then said, 'Will you use a bloody ashtray, why take it out on the plants?', and he can't understand why. He says, 'You treat them like kids', 'Well,' I says, 'they're special to me'.

SW What about the view from the window, you know, you were talking about the clock and the bend in the road and so on? Do you find your view is important to you?

Mr S Yes, as soon as I was offered this place, as soon as I walked in and I saw how bright, and I saw the view I said, 'Yes, I'm going to have this, this is fantastic'. I get a view, I'm not boxed in, it's open space. I like to see the planes, sometimes they take off in this direction, in a week when it's bloody freezing, and you see a plane and you say, 'I wonder if that's going to some place really nice and warm, lucky sods' and that, or in the summer when you see them coming back you think they've probably been to the Mediterranean where there's sun, and now they're back in England looking at that sky; you can't see a bit of blue.

SW You don't ever feel cut off from outside?

Mr S No, actually it's very, very peaceful. When I tell people I live in a tower block and all that, they say 'What about the noise?', I must say it's so quiet it's unbelievable. I've got three smashing neighbours, nobody bothers you, and we're all friendly. We take it in turns to do the hallway and everything like that; I couldn't ask for better people.

Penny Hearn

SW What about some of the objects then, this fish tank for instance, what does that really mean to you?
PH It's just something I find very relaxing to look at. I find it very interesting to get so many different fish and that; the little ones the colours and that sort of thing are nice to sit and look at – very soothing.

SW You find it sort of relieves tension?
PH Well, yes, I suppose it does when you think about it, I tend to drop asleep if I look at that too long.

SW So if you feel wound up or something . . .
PH I sit and look at the fish tank and have a cigarette, yes. I think it's because you stop thinking about everything that's going on, you're watching the fish more, it takes your mind off of whatever it is that's buggin' you.

SW Do you think the fish tank's a bit like you in your flat in a way, like it's another stage on, here you are sitting in your sort of place . . .
PH There's them in their little home, yes. In a way, I feel sorry for them, looking out at us, they're obviously aware that we're here.

SW Do you think you could feel claustraphobic in one of these rooms?
PH Well I never have. 'Cos I've got the balcony I can always open the door. Without a balcony I don't think I could be very happy living here.

SW Yes, but then a balcony's only the physical thing of going outside, why is that so different do you think?
PH I don't know, I think when you go out there and you've got the breeze on your face and everything it makes me feel much freer.

Mr and Mrs Small

SW You collect all these miniatures, can you tell me a little bit about them?
Mrs S Yes, they've come from various places,

we've got some from Russia, some from Poland, Majorca, Italy, Spain, lots of them come from Jersey. We don't just see them in a supermarket and buy them, it's places we've visited that these come from, or that friends have visited.

SW *So they're all mementoes of other places?*
Mrs S Yes, that's right, well they are all mementoes from some other place, lots of them we've got from Jersey, haven't we?
Mr S And friends have brought them back from places they've been to. We were in Spain and brought some back, we brought them back from Jersey and various places.
Mrs S I think most of them are from places like Spain and Jersey. We've been to Jersey about eight or nine times.

SW *Would you say, when you looked at them, they remind you of these other places?*
Mrs S Yes, that's right, yes; the good times we've had.
Mr S You look back, you look at them and think, I remember seeing them and we haven't got that, we'll get that, so it goes on.
Mrs S It's difficult when you go to these places to try and remember the ones you've got, 'cos you can end up with several doubles.

SW *So does it enlarge life in the flat in a way, because it gives you memories of outside?*
Mr S It does, yes. You sit there and reminisce of all the places we have been to, you look at them: 'Where did I buy that one now, and, oh yes, I bought that in so and so'.

SW *Do you feel you need things to get you out of here psychologically as well as spiritually?*
Mr S See that's why I borrow all these little gadgets like televisions and videos and all that to spend more time. If the weather's not very nice I can spend a whole day indoors mucking about, recording and things.

SW *You mean it gets you out into the world?*
Mr S I mean if you've got a teledisc you can have sports, it's entirely different from just having the television on all day; you can put on the teletext, for example.

I've got my day off pat, because you need a routine. I have to go by their timetable which means getting them up on time so they can get to school on time, which leaves the day free to cook, clean and what have you. Then collect them, then its eats, T.V. reading, homework, bed. Babysitters aren't falling over themselves, so I don't go out much.

I CAN SEE MORE GREEN THAN MOST PEOPLE, BUT THERE'S NO WAY YOU CAN TOUCH THE TREES OR GREENERY OR FEEL THAT THEY'RE THERE, THEY'RE OUTSIDE OF YOU, BUT INDOORS YOU CAN TOUCH THEM AND TEND THEM.

Sometimes I imagine I'm going along a country road, 'cos I would like to have a go on a bike on the real road, but usually I might put on a pop record, and it helps me keep pedalling. I just get on my bike and I keep looking at the clock to see how far I've got to go. I suppose I just sit and think about what I've got to do when I get off it, like start the dinner. or some other boring household chore.

Display boards from Brentford Towers,
October/November 1985

123

From a Walk to the Supermarket

Highfields Estate, situated on the outer reaches of West London at Feltham, had long been of interest to me as a symbol of the 'modern world', before I worked with Linda Hutchinson in the late 1980s. On a reconnaissance tour of West London in the mid-1970s I came across the estate accidentally, and had immediately responded to its monumentality and overall size and wanted to start work there at once. I was somewhat inhibited by the sheer brutality of the surroundings and it was to take me several years before I felt comfortable enough to develop a work. In 1978 I made the triptych *A Conflict of Identities*, centring on the relationship between an individual's reality on the estate, and an idealised projected image they desired to emulate in the form of wanting to be a professional photographic model.

I revisited the estate in 1988 to start on a new engagement with its residents, this time to initiate an installation to be situated in one of the buildings, *Multi-Storey Mosaic* (1990). By that time there had been a considerable negative transformation in people's attitudes about living there. The whole estate was constructed on site by factory assembled system, and as with similar projects it was intended to be a much larger and grander development, but had been truncated by lack of finance and a change in the political vision.

One of the intentions of *Multi-Storey Mosaic* was to bring together residents in pairs who had not met before, to construct a sequence of display boards featuring photographs and texts made by the participants, that were to be presented on the landings of the stairwell of Homecourt, the principal building at the estate centre. As part of this process a resident introduced me to Linda Hutchinson as a neighbour they thought would be interested in my ideas. From my first discussion it became apparent to me that Linda's fight to develop herself intellectually, and to create the life she wanted to live, overcame the potential restrictions of a single parent family with her three boys and formed a highly important, relevant cultural message.

The resulting work is structured over three panels formed from an actual walk we took, starting in the kitchen of Linda Hutchinson's flat in Hunter House, and progressing down the corridors, through the estate, to the local supermarket on Feltham High Street. This walk was seen by her to epitomise a day in her 'everyday' life and I asked her to locate along the way for me different groups of signs, which on one hand denoted the determinism of her situation in that environment, and on the other were agents of resistance and creative self-expression, a counter-consciousness. We took several walks, all along the same route, and each time I asked her to locate different signs in the fabric of the environment, which I photographed while and tape recorded her commentary about what we were confronting. She decided how she should be photographed and presented in the work.

Linda Hutchinson, 10 January 1990

SW I'm sitting in Linda Hutchinson's flat in Hunter House, on the Highfields Estate, and to start with I just thought we'd have a general conversation about this flat. So, this room, the way I experience it anyway, seems to naturally merge out into a view of the landscape which somehow you can't escape, it's always present. It must be very familiar, so tell me about it – when you go to that window are there things that really mean something to you?

LH Well, when I look out of the window now I realise how much it has changed, you know they've built a lot of houses where there used to be fields, there's a pig farm and a horse field; that's all still there. I mean I don't know whether that's going to be moved at a later date, but that's all still there. Obviously there's an estate on the other side of the railway tracks, so I tend to look in there and see what the people are doing, looking at them to see if anything has changed.

SW Do you feel almost familiar with them?

LH Yeah, I mean obviously from having seen them for all these years you sort of know who they are, and you just watch them. You don't see them everyday, you might see them once a week – not even that – but you do know who they are, where they live, and what they're doing, just from visual behaviour.

SW Do you imagine what they might be like?

LH Yeah, I mean occasionally, I mean the ones that live here, I can see down the High Street, I know who they are. It just seems funny that I can see into their houses and watch them, then I see them down the street; they don't know me, but I know who they are.

SW So you know things about them that they don't know that you know?

LH You see people fighting and arguing in their gardens in the summer and then you see them down the road and you know they've had an argument.

SW So, you've made the landscape personal to you because you know all these people. Do you feel distant from it somehow physically, or mentally?

LH Well, physically. I suppose if you live in a house you can just sort of walk out of your door into it, but living eight floors up in the air it's a sheer drop down, you're just watching, that's what it's like all the time, you're just watching, there is nothing you can do about it except watch. If you saw anything terrible happen, you couldn't just run out of your door and help, because you start eight floors up in the air, and there's nothing you can do about that, you're just watching all the time, that's all.

SW So what about the doll, it's very beautifully presented, unquestionably the whole centrepiece of the room, so tell me about this doll, why do you think you were drawn it?

LH I don't know, I just love that doll. I actually went to this exhibition with the school, my daughter's school, saw the doll there, and I went back the next day because they were making them there, there and then, and I got it, and I just like it.

SW Do you think it says something about you?

LH I like dolls and toys and things. I don't know whether I am escaping back into my childhood, lost childhood, I don't know, I keep thinking that's what it is, I keep buying things like that. Never used to be drawn towards anything like that, but the last couple of years, anything I see, that attracts my attention to do with little dolls or toys, I buy it.

SW But there's a lot of these things, so they must be your expression of yourself?

LH They must be, that's what I'm saying, because I messed up my childhood I am reverting back into it, kind of relive it now, just by buying things to make me feel, I don't know, I suppose they are around me to comfort me you know. The bedroom is the same, it's full of stuffed toys and dolls and . . .

SW Do you think what you're doing is making a creative statement: this is a very square flat, and it must be the same as all the others, so somehow you've got to do something here?

LH This is me, this is what I'm working

towards. As I said to you, when the kids were young they were my life, you know, bringing them up, but as you get older, I've changed with it and I'm developing interest in all sorts of things, even if it's just buying things like that, whereas I was never interested before, but something in me is changing and I feel drawn towards that.

SW *Do you feel that you want to change the space of the flat by what you are doing?*
LH Also, I've lived here so long now, it became very boring. I've decorated quite a bit, changed it quite a bit, to the way I really want it now, which is totally different to anything I wanted before.

SW *But do you see some objects like this thing here with the ice cream, this fantasy, do you see it as a mentally freeing thing, when you look at that does it free you somehow?*
LH Well. I don't know. I did actually want that myself, but I felt I couldn't buy it for myself, I would feel stupid buying that, so I thought, right, I'll buy it for my daughter, that way I've got it, it's not mine but I can still look at it. I felt better buying it for a child than for me.

SW *Thinking about the way you painted it and arranged all these pictures around. How do you think you're breaking up the space?*
LH Well, these are plain rooms so, I don't know, something happened and I thought I want pictures everywhere, but the pictures that I wanted as I said were children, all of children; old fashioned children and ghost children, and things like that. I just had this obsession with children and toys, whereas I didn't with my own kids when they were younger, I mean I was a good mother and everything but I don't know, something has changed in me that has made me want all this sort of thing around me.

SW *You're eight floors up in the sky – do you think that affects the relationships and things like that, being in a contained environment?*
LH Yes, it does, from season to season, it has its advantages anyway. In the winter if you live in a house the kids can't go out at all, in the winter here they can go out in the corridor, they can play ball games, it doesn't matter what the weather's like outside, a bit more freedom that way. I suppose it does, it restricts him because he feels . . . if you've got a front door to walk out of, but sometimes I say to him, just go out, 'Oh, I can't be bothered, I've got to call the lift, walk down the stairs. Especially if the lifts are out, then he can't be bothered, and he just won't go so, yes, it's restricting in that way.

SW *But does that affect you at all, this journey to the outside you have to make everytime?*
LH Sometimes I feel I can't be bothered, oh I'll go tomorrow. It depends especially with the lifts; if they're not working you think you've got to walk down eight flights of stairs, do your shopping and then walk up eight flights of stairs. Yes, it puts you off.

SW *When you go shopping do you feel that you would want to be doing something else?*
LH I don't go to the shops that often. If I don't go to the shops my daily routine is more boring. I go to the shops to break the routine, I do sometimes go to the shops just to get out, because apart from the shops there is nothing else to do, apart from housework.

SW *Do you budget your life quite well?*
LH I do budget my life, I budget my money – moments of frivolousness and that – but no, I budget my money. I have to, so I do it, it became a way of life and I've got a bit more money now, but I still live like that.

SW *You must have had quite a lot of difficult times, so you feel life is a bit easier than it was in the past?*
LH Oh God, yes, but then I am a stronger person now. I have always been self-sufficient that way but I am a lot more now, I find it very hard now in a personal relationship which I've got with somebody, I find it very hard to let them do things with me, I become really independent, probably to a fault.

SW *The other thing I found interesting was that you were doing this course, do you think* that is an attempt to change your life, to exert more influence over what you're doing?

LH The reason I did this sociology course was because it was a topic, a course of all different aspects of life, a lot of them which I was interested in anyway, but not everybody is, so to be able to go there, talk about it with people that are interested in it as well, like write about what you feel, rather than have to bore someone who is not really interested is another 'self' thing it was what I wanted to do what I want to talk about

SW Do you think it brings out your potential?
LH I felt as if my brain was going to rot, I felt I wasn't doing anything with my brain. I have to use it in my job obviously, which I do, I've got a lot of responsibility there that other people don't get, but saying that, it's not enough. It's not enough for me, so I felt I had to do that, it made my brain work. I do crosswords every-day, things like that, read, it wasn't enough, I just felt I had to do more.

3 May 1990

SW Do you have a lot to do with people around you, I mean in this block?
LH Next door neighbour, that's about it.

SW It's not really a social environment?
LH It used to be when I first lived here, everyone up here had little kids, we used to sort of sit out in the corridor with them and they used to run around, but I mean they've all grown up and moved and I don't really have anything to do with anyone. A couple of girls down the end of the corridor, one of them had a couple of little girls that I like, so they spend a lot of time with us, that's about it.

SW I've got the feeling from what you've been saying that there have been big changes in your life, and you've gradually got more and more organised.
LH Well, yes, I have. My private life is off the estate, whereas I can look out of this window and look down and I know most of the people that live underneath me in those little blocks,

I FIND IT VERY HARD NOW
IN A PERSONAL RELATIONSHIP TO LET ANYONE SHARE

MY LIFE REVOLVES AROUND IRONING
WASHING, IRONING, CLEANING, WASHING

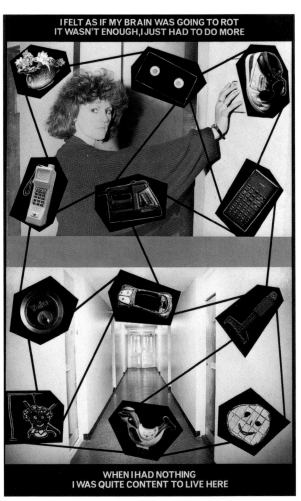

I FELT AS IF MY BRAIN WAS GOING TO ROT
IT WASN'T ENOUGH, I JUST HAD TO DO MORE

WHEN I HAD NOTHING
I WAS QUITE CONTENT TO LIVE HERE

their life is the estate, and it's like a little ghetto, that's the way it is over there, their life is that: in and out of each other's houses, I couldn't live like that, it would crack me up.

SW Because you were saying you didn't know whether you were trying to re-create your childhood.
LH Well, I don't know re-creating, making. I didn't have, I was never encouraged to have dolls, I had dolls bought for me, but never to keep them all, be feminine. They just wanted

me to go to school and be academic.

SW Get out of the way?
LH No, not to get out of the way, go to university, that sort of thing. Everything was school, school, school, homework, homework, homework. If I didn't get any homework they would give me homework, never to collect things or nothing like that, so I never really had that.

SW So you were a sort of rebel then?

LH Oh God, yeah, terrible, down and out, through and through, as my Dad said, and hasn't spoken to me since. I just didn't want to live the way they wanted me to live, I didn't want to do what they wanted me to do, I didn't see why I should do it and that was that.

SW *Do you think there is a period of your life when you are open to influence and you become who you are, in the past?*
LH I suppose so, I can't think when that was with me, probably about two years ago, I became who I am and that's the way I am going to stay I think. That's when I finally grew up, after my marriage blew up and everything. It wasn't actually growing up, it's realising there is more to life than that, and that I'd had enough. It made me give myself a kick up the ass, and that was it, I think I've been the same since then.

From a Walk to the Supermarket, *April/October 1990, three panel work, 78cm wide by 128cm high. Photographic prints, photographic dye, acrylic paint and Letraset text, mounted on paper and card*

Signs and Messages from Corporate America

The proliferation of whole systems of signs that tell us what to do or who we are, is a largely unannounced feature of urban life today. A feature of this quietly spreading network of institutionally originated signs is their inherent reductiveness in the basic representation of complex reality. These institutional signs form a 'secret language', articulated somewhere out of reach of those whom it affects. A contrast in language is formed from highly personal expression, made public by people under pressure from the various forms of institutional signs. It takes the form of sign systems that manifest the self-identity, community and creative power of the sign maker. It is subversive, and often consists of spontaneous layerings made directly on to the very physical surfaces that that radiate messages of institutional determinism. Here I include the material structure of the environment, for example, wood panelling, polished marble and unpainted concrete. Personal, informal sign systems originate undercover, as a counter-consciousness jumping out from behind the fabric to demand attention.

The polemic created between formal, reductive signs and informal, expansive signs which share a common presence within the day-to-day time span, provides an important means of viewing that experience. In my interpretation of Olympia & York's invitation to participate in their exhibition of installations *The Urban Landscape* – conceived as a celebration for the opening of the World Financial Center in Battery Park, New York, 1988 – I sought to create a direct link with the building in which my work was to be presented.

The Center presented symbols of corporate power that I could embody in my piece, and which were festooned with a multiplicity of sign systems, relevant and readily comprehended by the primary audience; the office workers within. I constructed a mosaic of signs into a seemingly chaotic surface, with some of the real-life counterparts present only twenty feet away. In this respect, to further open up my mosaic of signs, I extended it to include another dimension; a montage of audio signs recorded from various pieces of office equipment – air conditioning, computer keyboards, radio-paging devices, lift announcements – all located inside the Merrill Lynch building.

I documented sign systems on the inside: those belonging to the desktop of two people situated within a small open-plan office space dedicated to the maintenance of that same building. I asked the staff who sat at those desks everyday to identify the different visual and audio sign systems that coexisted in the space directly in front of them. Although each desk was the same, and the staff were given much the same working equipment, each desk was quite different, with people bringing various objects into that space stating their individualism, and at the same time psychologically projected them out of that desk environment into the world outside.

Cathy Gagliardi and Maryanne Mahlen,
24 August 1988

SW So, let's talk about this environment you're in really, it's an open-plan, typical office environment. How do you feel when you come in every morning and you turn the corner and there's that little set of boxes there?
CG I just think there it goes again, another day.
MM I feel the same way. It's sometimes a lot of fun with the people that work here, but the environment itself is extremely stressful, demanding. There is no privacy in the open area, the way we are situated, and it's just a constant flow of traffic where we are. It's an extremely hectic, chaotic area.
CG Loud, very loud area, between the walkie-talkies and the phones ringing off the wall, people complaining in our ears.
MM Constantly. That's what we have, a constant flow of complaints. We manage the whole building and it's just either too cold, or too hot, a leak, ceiling's moving, the lights are out, move my plants they're dead, they're dying. It's just a constant flow of traffic with our engineers, our carpenters, it's just never-ending until we leave at the end of the day.

SW But do you find that the open-plan system is very noisy, you were saying about noise?
MM Yes, it's extremely stressful because there is no privacy, if you're on a phone on a complaint call you can have five people standing behind your cubicle talking, and it's extremely distracting. That makes you more stressful because you try to hear someone yelling at you complaining, and then you're hearing other people talking and to hear four different conversations it's chaotic, it's just very stressful. And you go home on the trains and it's more stress, and then you go home and that's where it ends.

SW Do you manage to cut out the other people's noise, I mean just attend to what you're dealing with?
MM I find that difficult to do that where I'm located, being the first cubicle, there's a lot of influx there, close to the men's facilities and its constant flow. It's like they're gathering

there all the time and where I sit it's very distracting.

SW *Can you keep a kind of contact with the outside?*

MM Yes, you have to. If you don't have the outside world you just can't accomplish your life here, because this whole environment is a complaint area, and you just think of twelve hours a day of listening to nothing but complaints. We don't get, 'Oh thank you, oh that's wonderful, oh terrific'; we get screamed at, we get yelled at, we get demanded upon, we get, I mean I've got verbally abused many times and so has Cathy.

SW *I noticed that there's a lot what we call banter between you all in the office, do you think that's helped by the open plan?*

MM No, 'cos I used to be in an office and we had the same banter, the same joking around. Cathy had a much more secluded cubicle, it's just more of a walk into it but you had seclusion, you had some privacy. You don't have that here, I indicate my cubicle as a driveway, that's exactly what it represents to me, you drive in and you drive out, there's no, you know, it's just very un-private and I feel in an office environment you need privacy at times.

SW *Do you ever feel you can express yourself?*

CG Definitely, I always express myself, if I'm mad I let everybody know, if I'm happy I let everybody know, if I'm sad I let everybody know. I usually express myself very well.

SW *You've both got lots of things around you from outside, from your home life or from holidays or whatever. What role do you think those things have for you?*

CG They're our personal things they make us feel like you're a little bit at home, like it gives you a little bit of feeling that it's not all work. You can look at something, you can look at the pictures that you have on your desk, and everything means something to you.

SW *There's two classes of objects there, the personal and the impersonal and they coexist in the same state.*

CG Exactly.

MM But I think everybody has a touch, you know, everything that is other than business, I had an award, that meant something to me, Cathy has an award, we display them because they were given from the company. My private pictures are something that I want to look at everyday, and I don't. I'm not home to look at them at home, and they give me good feelings because unicorns to me are mythical.

SW *Yes, I was going to ask why you were involved with unicorns.*

MM They're something unreal, and I sometimes like to dwell in the unreal, 'cos reality sometimes is, it's not good, and life sometimes deals us pretty bad hands and that life, that fantasy life that they come from, is so beautiful that I just like to dwell on it and look at them and it's, it's just a mythical life.

SW *Without these things you'd feel more anonymous?*

CG Yes, it's bad to go into a cubicle if there's nothing there, you have to have something of yourself.

MM The cubicle itself is not warm, so you have to make it warm. When I first moved here I cried because I was so sad about the way it looked; it was so cold and we were facing the other way at the time, they had moved us around. It's different now. You have to make it warm, because it's a cold environment.

CG Make it a part of you.

SW *Do you find it important to have people present, like you've got people talking to you on the phone, people coming on the radio?*

CG No, no, I'd rather have someone. These people are your friends, you consider them your friends, you sit and you talk, you know, it's good to have someone.

MM The only people we talk to on the phones . . . so when someone gives us a problem on the phone I'll go in to Cathy and I'll say 'Do you know what this lady just said?' and I'll say a few choice words and she does the same. Joey'll get mad and slam the phone down and say, 'I can't believe this person just said this to me', it's life, working, you know, in this area.

SW *Going back to the objects on your desk, can you tell me what you feel are the most significant ones to the work that you're doing?*
MM The phone.
CG It'd have to be the phone.

SW *So, when that phone rings, you kind of go into automatic response?*
CG Grrrr! You want to kill.
MM It drives you crazy when you're alone or if you're shorthanded, and you have a leak here, an electrical problem there, and you can't leave the desk. You have to get a response and people aren't calling you. That's happened to everyone of us, where you literally want to pull your hair out of your head and you can't wait for five o'clock, just to leave, I've had plenty of times like that, I know Cathy has.
CG Yes, surely, you think about personal things that are happening to you, you think about boyfriends, about family, everything that happens, it's daydreaming, and, the next minute you go back to what you were doing.
MM Oh yes, we don't leave reality for too lengthy a time, because the phone'll ring and you're right back to square one.

SW *Do you sometimes take on a corporate identity, I mean, do you become another person when you open the door?*
MM When I go to outside meetings, not here.
CG I don't think I do. People say I sound different, my sister will tell me I change my whole voice, she says I sound like I'm being too nice over the phone, but I don't think so, I think I sound the same.

SW *I just wondered if the language changed?*
MM Well, you're pleasant on the phone to people, you have to be. That's what we're told and regardless of even the response that you might get from the person on the phone, you still have to be pleasant. You might not be as pleasant when you hang up the phone, but you cannot vent it on the people on the phone because they'll complain and call your boss and they're always right. It's like everything else, the pedestrian is always right, the people here, the client is always right.

Signs and Messages from Corporate America, *August/September 1988, twenty-three panel work, varying in size from Letraset text, mounted on card. Installation presented with a six-minute audio cassette loop*

92.5cm high by 139cm wide to 62cm wide by 41cm high. Photographic prints, photographic dye, acrylic paint,

Personal Islands

Personal Islands centred on the relativity of people's perception of their living environment and the expressive role objects played in that personal environment. The work was made with the participation of two groups of residents from two buildings on opposite sides of the Isle of Dogs in East London: Kelson House on the Samuda Estate and Top Mast Point on the Barkentine Estate. With each participant I took photographs and recorded discussions, centred on the significance that objects had in their personal life inside the flat. The work was developed to form two installations situated in the entrance foyers of Kelson House and Top Mast Point, and was viewed with the aid of *The Personal Islands*, a book given to anyone wishing to visit them as a means of creating connections between the two environments. Each installation consisted of five freestanding display boards comprising photographs and texts made directly from the documentations with residents.

Shelley and Paul Twin, 24 May 1992

SW *If you could cast your minds back to when you first knew you'd got this flat, what were the first thoughts that came through your heads?*

PT I'd already been, I visited here when it was first built. I came and visited with some friends when I was fifteen and I'd always lived in a house low down, so when I came to this place and come up right to the top of the upper floors and walked in, the place was completely different to anything I'd been in, because you went in and you went down everywhere, the bedrooms were downstairs, everything was upside down and as I walked out it was night and I looked out and there was suddenly like this amazing view with a mass of lights and I'd never looked at London in that way. When I came back I was quite looking forward to it, that memory stayed with me but then when I visited here twenty years later, when I moved in things had changed a bit.

SW *But you have set about doing something in this flat, haven't you, you haven't allowed the flat to dictate, you've actually tried to create an environment?*

PT That's right. I wanted to put a sort of, I know it's a cliché, but my own personality on the place.

SW *Could you tell us a bit about what you've tried to do?*

PT I had a mad idea to lay a different floor. I didn't want just ordinary carpets so I laid a terrazzo floor, which means that basically you've never got to do anything to it. It doesn't get dirty, it doesn't matter what you chuck on it, you just wipe, mop it up and it's clean again and you can carry on from there. Of course it has drawbacks, it's fairly cold; in the summer it's lovely and cool. The ash skirting is just a whim I had, I knew about the idea that the ash tree was symbolic of the world in old Germanic literature, it appears in Baden all the time and that's one of my hobbies. I just wanted to bring ash into the room and use it as a symbol to root the place to the ground and so I decided that all the wood in the place

should be ash; that everything in here should just be natural – stone, timber – and then the other objects that'd be here were really supposed to be just things that were functional, so there'd be ash bookshelves, but there wouldn't be things there as ornaments, they'd either be things that we used, or they'd be the real basic material of the home, and that was it.

SW *So would you say that you were trying to sort of counter the physicality of the block?*

PT Yes, but changing the fabric itself so that the fabrics here wouldn't really just be concrete and coverings, that they'd be deeper than that by actually having a proper stone floor, and by having proper timber rather than the sort of synthetic skirtings that you get in normal council houses.

SW *Would you say there was an identity here, like people sort of say 'I come from Kelson'?*

PT Yeah they do, I think. People do seem to identify with this place. One of the things about it is because the way it stands out, it's all on its own on the edge of the river like a great big monolith that just sticks out above the rest of the buildings around here, so you do visually identify with it very easily, when you're travelling home on the Docklands Light Railway.

SW *Do you think people have come together here because of the negative aspects of the environment?*

PT I think the reason eventually they've had to come together is because they've realised that nobody's going to do anything for them, even people who profess that they're going to do something for themselves, and gradually that's what happened. They realised that the only way they were going to get anything done was if they go out, just agitate and make sure that it gets done themselves. They can't really trust it to other people, because the interest you have if you live there is profound, it doesn't end at five o'clock and too often that's what happens when you leave it to someone else.

Nick Harrison, 10 June 1992

SW Do you have much to do with people living around you?
NH Well, since the security systems and they've spent more money on the estate to improve the quality of life here, the security doors and stuff, the community has as far as I'm concerned, it has kind of blossomed since, and I've got a few friends, not a lot, a few friends in Kelson House, but on the island I've got quite a few friends and the nice thing about going to visit your friends in Kelson House is that you don't have to worry if it's like pissing down outside because you can go in you shorts and t-shirt because you're just going to get into the lift and go to whatever floor they live on, and you don't have to worry about getting a taxi home or anything, but that's extremely limited. I do have quite a few friends that live around the Isle of Dogs, but I've lived here for ten years and so you naturally sort of build up friends in the area.

Kay Morris, 23 June 1992

SW Do you feel there's something in that landscape that you really connect with?
KM I don't know what it is about the view, it's just a gorgeous view and I suppose there's always something going on, I mean the helicopters, you think they're going to land on the roof when they come over, and a few boats that go up and down. Now I've got the dog I can look out and see if there's any of his friends down there so I can take him down to play with his friends rather than take him down when there's no one there. I just love this view, that we are up this high and we can come in and shut that door and that's it, there's no interruptions, there's just nothing it's just great.

SW Do you feel that you've sort of created your own capsule in here?
KM I think so, yes, and yet I like company. My door's open all the time, if anyone wants to come in they're welcome, I enjoy people coming in. But as I say, Don, my husband,

doesn't, so if I do invite people up it's during the day when he's not here.

SW Have you set about trying to create a particular atmosphere in here?
KM No I'm not a homemaker, not in any sense of the word. I don't even put curtains up, mainly because I think it spoils the view, but it does look bare. I know it looks bare when you come in 'cos there's no curtains up.

SW Do you find you have a lot to do with people in the block, is there a sense of community?
KM No, very little. The people I speak to are the people who've got dogs and we meet downstairs. There's people on this floor have been here twenty years and in fact there's only a couple that I've ever actually been inside their house, inside their flat.

SW Could you say how life has changed in the twenty years you've been here?
KM Basically, I don't think it's changed at all, I get the feeling from talking to people that the islanders, as they call themselves, resent the change, a lot of them anyway.

SW No I mean the block.
KM In the block, apart from it going from bad to worse, I mean, they've started putting children up here again which is bad. There's too much graffiti, too many dirty people that throw their rubbish out, I don't care what their homes are like, as you can see from mine I'm not a homemaker, and as I said before, I loathe housework, but you don't throw your rubbish out of your windows and you don't make life unpleasant for other people, but in this block there's an awful lot of them do, so really it hasn't improved at all. I suppose it must be the last year if I think about it, it's not all that long ago since all this started, maybe five years ago that we started really getting problems, I don't think it goes back much further than that and I don't know why it happened except that it was a hard-to-let block and they put in problem families. A lot of people blame the fact that there's Pakis and Bangladeshis and boat people and all the rest

of it, I can't say that, I don't know. I honestly don't think they're any worse than the white people, in fact I think it's white people that do all this throwing the muck out of the windows, and of course the teenagers. I took the dog down today and there's loads of empty beer cans, and that's another thing – the place isn't cleaned properly, we've only got one decent cleaner, Tony, and from the state of the place this week I don't think he's on duty because all this would be cleared up.

SW *So it needs maintenance all the time?*
KM Yeah, the cleaners – as far as I'm concerned – are useless. If you have to walk down these stairs if the lifts aren't working they really stink to high heaven because they're used as toilets, the stairs as well, and I just think something could be done about it.

SW *Would you like to have that contact with outside?*
KM In fine weather unless you're prepared to traipse downstairs and go over there there's nowhere you can go to get a bit of sunshine. Balconies would be lovely, but they won't do it, they're knocking in new windows supposedly, I don't know when.

Fred and John Harris, 30 June 1992

SW *Did you see this concrete building as a symbol of modern life?*
FH Well, I thought myself when you come up into these places, you walk in and you go click click click and you don't know anybody. But we talk to Kay and that, we talk to her husband and the dog when he's there, stroke the dog and make friends.

SW *You're right at the top of the building – do you sometimes feel like you're sitting on top of everybody else?*
FH No, no, but when we had that terrible wind and you sit here and you look out the window and you set your eyes on a point and sitting there then like that, and you can feel that sway because the building will move. Every high building has got to move, you know, but we've

been sitting here at night times and heard 'crack' and then hear a crack run across the floor, it could be the drying out of the building, it's so old.

JH That's very nice usually isn't it? It's in that corner?

FH Yes, it makes a funny noise . . .

SW Really?

FH And different things. It cracks, but I've spoke to people in this block . . .

JH If it goes, it goes.

FH I've spoke to people in this block and when they first moved into this thing, when it was first opened, the doors used to open, well, once the doors was open they could shut 'em easy, but now they can't shut the doors 'cos the frames are twisted.

SW So do you think life has changed much in East London, since you've been here?

FH Oh yes, changed a lot since they done that horrible building across the road there, Canary Wharf.

JH Not much of the docks left now are there?

FH No, if you see that building, they turned round and said when they got that going, they said they was gonna have plenty of jobs for the likes of the boys on the island and I know a terrific load of lads on the island and they're still out of work, even when that was being built. They was going over to try and get jobs and they said no, you ain't got jobs because we've brought the boys from Ireland, Scotland, Germany, Wales, all from other countries to work on it, and the East End boys and all the Island boys couldn't get nothing, couldn't get the jobs.

Mick and Mandy Benson, 3 June 1992

SW When you first knew you were getting a flat here, what came through your minds?

Mick Well, we had mixed feelings really. When we first come into the block, you know, graffiti everywhere and the flat itself was left in a tip, there was black paint on the walls, gloss paint, and we were shocked and devastated at the way the flat looked, but at the same time

we was happy because we didn't have a flat to share for ourselves. So we were going to start a new life together and get married and we was looking forward to what we could do to the flat.

SW So you were optimistic really?

Mandy We were just happy that we were going to be together weren't we? Because we were separate until we got the flat, yeah.

Mick We was optimistic in a way, looking at all the good things we could do to the flat, all the changes we could make and what it would look like when we did clean and paint it up.

SW Right from the start you had not exactly a vision, but an idea of what you could do to it?

Mick Mandy's quite artistic, so she imagined all the plants everywhere and what colour she wanted the walls and everything, so yeah, we was optimistic in a way.

SW What sort of atmosphere did you set about trying to create in here?

Mandy We wanted to bring the outside in, you know, like plants and make it all countri-fied and that type of thing.

Mick We put the flowered curtains up and the lead-like windows up there to make it have a nice country feel and that was our aim; to cheer the place up and make it look nice and colourful. We are high up, and it's very hard to get out of the block, the lifts break down quite often and it's not simple like walking out your street door and you've got fresh air, it's quite a nuisance going out so we had to bring the outside in.

SW In a way you seem to be saying it's slightly introverted being in here, but are you conscious of other people around you?

Mick In the block? Yeah, we are, but you'd think living in a block like this you'd know everyone and you'd see people quite a lot, but you don't. You hear doors slamming and unlocking, it's like a prison at times, it sounds like that, but you don't really know people well.

Mandy We've got eight other people on the landing, and sometimes you never see them for weeks.

SW *You've been here five years now – has your relationship changed with the place and the people in that time?*

Mick I think when we first come, because I'm not from this area – I'm from Stepney and Mandy's from Carlisle – it seemed quite a rough area and the people seemed aloof.

Mandy It was quite cliquey, you'd get these people just staring at you, as if to say, this is a new face.

Mick It was quite unnerving at times, wasn't it? We've been here five years now, and although we don't talk to that many people we're friendly and we're sort of accepted and you feel part of the area. You think people don't notice you but they do. If you go missing, that's when they start asking questions, and then when they see you every day they don't talk to you. It's like they're embarrassed to talk to you or frightened they're gonna get a funny response, you know.

SW *I noticed these weights – are there things you've got here that somehow compensate for the fact that you can't extend out physically?*

Mick Yes, I used to go training three or four times a week and because of the hardship of getting to Aldgate and back, I've had to bring weights into the house, and we're both interested in getting fit, but it's just getting round to it regularly. That's another thing the block's stopped me doing, because it's in such an awkward place.

SW *In a way, the physicality of the block inhibits you from expressing yourself physically?*

Mandy Yeah, because we'd like to do jogging and it's just so hard. You go out jogging, to come back you've got to get in the lift, you're sweaty and other people are in this lift and just to come back in from jogging, it's just . . .

Mick We did try it before and then we tried mountain bikes, And even that was a hardship, getting them in the lifts and in the flat, so you're really quite restricted: whatever you do, you've really got to do it in the flat.

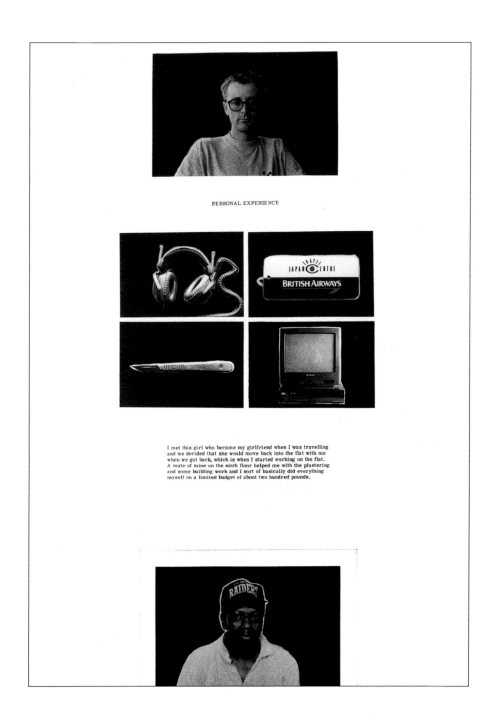

Display boards from Personal Islands, *February 1993*

PERSONAL IMAGINATION

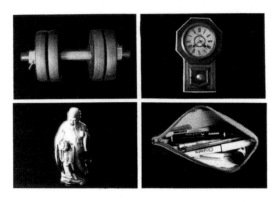

We put the flowered curtains up and the lead-like windows up
there to make it have a country feel, and as we are high up and
it's quite a nuisance going out we had to bring the outside inside.
You can look out of the window and it's quite countrified, so we
tried to create that in the flat, but obviously there's only so far
you can go, we've got loads of plants everywhere and it's all
getting really big, it's becoming like a jungle.

Select Bibliography

Stafford Beer, *Decision and Control*, John Wiley & Sons (Chichester) 1966.

Kiesler and Kiesler, *Conformity*, Addison-Wesley Publishing Company (London) 1970.

Dale Lake, *Perceiving and Behaving*, Teachers' College Press, Columbia University (New York) 1970.

Marshall McLuhan, *The Medium is the Message*, Quentin Fiore, 1967.

— *The Mechanical Bride: Folklore of Industrial Man*, Routledge and Kegan Paul (London) 1967.

Mechanisation of Thought Process, proceedings of the symposium held at the National Physical Laboratory, Her Majesty's Stationery Office (London) 1958.

Allen Newell and Herbert A Simon, *Human Problem Solving*, Prentice-Hall, Englewood Cliffs (New Jersey/London) 1972.

Gordon Pask, *The Self-Organising System of a Decision-Making Group*, Third International Congress on Cybernetics, Association of International Cybernetics, 1965.

Harold Rosen, *Language and Class*, Falling Wall Press (Bristol) 1972.

Stephen Willats, *Art and Social Function*, Latimer New Dimensions (London) 1976.

— *Balcony*, Imprint (London) 1994.

— *Corridor*, Inschoot (Gent, Belgium) 1991.

— *Ich lebe in Einem Betonklotz*, Buchhandlung Walther Konig (Cologne) 1980.

— *Intervention and Audience*, Coracle Press (London) 1986.

— *Life Codes and Behaviour Parameters*, The Midland Group (Nottingham) 1976.

— *Living Within Contained Conditions*, MOMA (Oxford) 1978.

— *Society Through Art*, HCAK (The Hague, The Netherlands) 1990.

— *Stairwell*, Coracle Press (London) 1990.

— *The Artist as an Instigator of Changes in Social Cognition and Behaviour*, Gallery House Press (London) 1973.

— *The Lurky Place*, Lisson Gallery (London) 1978.

Catalogues and Archives

Conceptual Living, text by Stephen Bann, Victoria Miro Gallery (London) 1991.

Concerning Our Present Way of Living, Whitechapel Art Gallery (London) 1979.

Control Magazine, issues 1 to 15 published by Stephen Willats (London) since 1965.

Leben in Vogegbenen Grenzen – 4 Inseln in Berlin, Nationalgalerie Berlin, 1980-81.

Living Together, Tramway (Glasgow) 1995.

Secret Language, Corner House (Manchester) 1989.

Stephen Willats Printed Archive, from the holdings of the National Art Library at the Victoria and Albert Museum (London).

The New Reality, Orchard Gallery (Londonderry) 1982.